S0-CMS-752

IPHONE 14 PRO MAX USER GUIDE

A Complete Step By Step Instruction Manual for Beginners & Seniors to Learn How to Use the New iPhone 14 Pro Max With iOS Tips & Tricks

BY

HERBERT A. CLARK

Copyright © 2022 HERBERT A. CLARK

All rights reserved. No part of this book shall be reproduced, stored in a retrieval system, or transmitted by any means, electronic, mechanical, photocopying, recording, or otherwise, without written permission from the publisher. Although every precaution has been taken in the preparation of this book, the publisher and author assume no responsibility for errors or omissions. Nor is any liability assumed for damages resulting from the use of the information contained herein.

LEGAL NOTICE:

This book is copyright protected and is only for personal use. This book should not be amended or distributed, sold, quote, or paraphrased without the consent of the author or publisher.

Table of Contents

Page |

Page |

INTRODUCTION

Announced at Apple's event on September 7, the iPhone 14 Pro Max is Apple's most Advance smartphone ever. The new iPhone 14 Pro Max comes with a 6.7" OLED screen, an improved camera, a faster chip, better display capabilities, and more.

This year, Apple replaced the top notch with the Dynamic Island—a pill shaped cutout that morphs & changes shape to fit what's on your screen.

The iPhone 14 Pro Max is available in Space Black, Gold, Silver, & Purple.

What's in the Box

iPhone 14 Pro Max

USB-C to Lightning Cable

FEATURES OF IPHONE 14 PRO MAX

Design

The iPhone 14 Pro Max has an all-glass front & a matte glass back that covers a frame made from stainless steel.

Apple ditched the notch in the iPhone 14 Pro max model to introduce what it calls the Dynamic Island (A circular cutout and a pill-shaped cutout that morphs & changes shape to fit what is on your screen).

The iPhone 14 Pro Max is a 6.7" phone. It's 6.33" tall, 3.05" wide, 0.31" thick, and weighs 240g. it's available in dark purple, gold, space black & silver.

Display

The iPhone 14 Pro Max has a 2796 by 1290 pixel resolution. It also features an OLED Super Retina XDR screen. A 2,000,000:1 contrast ratio that supports brighter whites & darker blacks, and the screen has up to two thousand nits peak brightness when outside to make it easy to see the screen in the sun.

Wide colour support delivers clear, lifelike colours and True Tone matches the display's white balance to the lighting in your surroundings to provide a paper-like viewing experience that's pleasant to look at

The iPhone 14 Pro Max now has an Always-On display feature which keeps the screen on always without draining the battery. The Always-on Display feature darkens the wallpaper to give it a subtle look while keeping the time & widgets active on the lock screen

RAM

The iPhone 14 Pro Max has 6 GB RAM.

Storage space

Storage begins at 128 GB for the cheapest versions of the iPhone 14 Pro Max, but there are also 256 GB, 512 GB, and 1 TB options.

Camera

On the front, there is an f/1.9 aperture TrueDepth camera that offers better low-light performance pictures & videos.

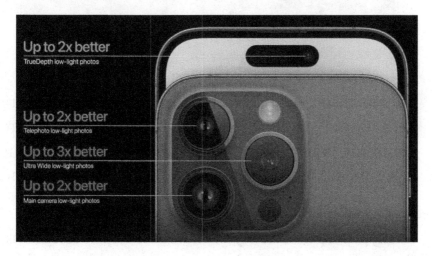

On the back of the iPhone 14 Pro Max, there is a 48-megapixel Wide lens that makes use of a 2nd-gen optical image sensor and has a focal length of 24mm and an aperture of f/1.78.

There's also a new Ultra Wide 12-megapixel camera with 1.4μm pixels for sharper pictures and more detail for macro photography. The Ultra Wide lens has a focal length of 13 mm, an f/2.2 aperture, and a 120-degree view field.

Lastly, there is a newly enhanced Telephoto camera that offers 3x optical zoom that can be used in conjunction with the 2x zoom available on the Wide camera. The 6-element lens has a focal length of 77 mm, an aperture of f/2.8, and support for optical image stabilization.

Battery life

The iPhone 14 Pro Max has a 4232mAh battery. It can last for about 29 hours when watching videos, about 25 hours when streaming videos, and about 95 hours when playing music. The device supports fast charging and can charge up to 50% in thirty minutes with a 20W or higher power adapter.

Emergency SOS via satellite

The iPhone 14 Pro Max can connect to a satellite in states of emergency when Wi-Fi & mobile connections are unavailable.

To make use of this new feature, you must be in an open area with few trees so that your device can connect to any available satellites in the sky.

Apple also created a user-friendly interface that walks you through how to connect your device to a satellite, and they have also designed a compressed messaging protocol because sending messages via satellite can take a few minutes.

Emergency SOS provides some questions that you need to answer when it's activated, these questions aim to quickly obtain important info needed by emergency personnel, and your answers are then sent to emergency services.

iPhone 14 Pro Max users can also use satellite connectivity to update their Find My location while hiking or camping off the grid.

Crash Detection

If your phone detects a car accident, it can help in contacting emergency services & notifying your emergency contacts.

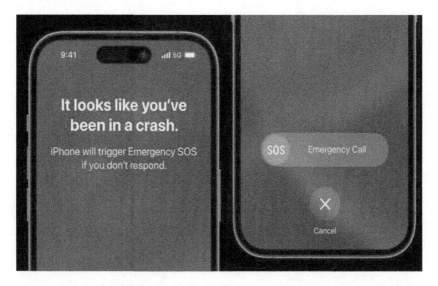

When your iPhone detects a serious accident in your car, it will show a notification and automatically start calling emergency services after 20 seconds if you don't cancel the alert. If you do not respond, your phone will send a voice message to emergency services, informing them that you have been involved in a serious accident and it will also send them your longitudinal & latitudinal coordinates.

SET UP YOUR IPHONE

Switch on your phone

Long-press the side button on your iPhone until the screen displays the Apple logo.

Then you will see "Hello" in different languages. Adhere to the directives on your screen to begin setup.

Setup manually or use Quick-Start

You can use the Quickstart feature to automatically setup your new iPhone if you have another device.

If you do not have other devices, touch the **Setup Manually** button.

Activate your iPhone

Your iPhone must be connected to a WiFi or cellular network to activate and proceed with the setup.

Touch a WiFi network (if available) to connect to it, or touch the **Continue without Wi-Fi** button to utilize your iPhone's mobile network.

Setup Face ID & create a passcode

Adhere to the directives on your display to setup Face ID so that you would be able to unlock your device & authenticate purchases with your face.

After that, enter a 6-digit code to protect your data. A passcode is required to use features like Face ID, Apple Pay, etc. Touch **Passcode Options** to see more options.

Restore or transfer your applications & data

Touch how you want to move your data from your old device to your iPhone.

If there's no available backup or if you do not other devices, touch **Don't Transfer Applications and data.**

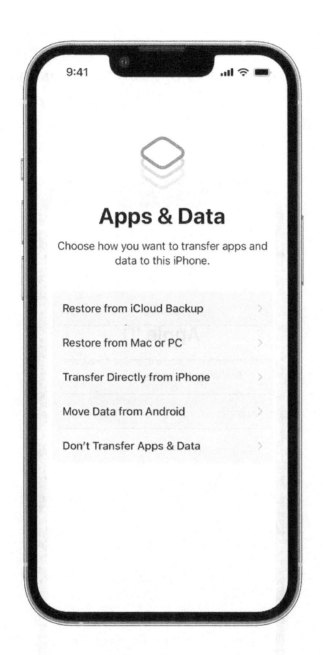

Apps & Data

Choose how you want to transfer apps and data to this iPhone.

Restore from iCloud Backup >

Restore from Mac or PC >

Transfer Directly from iPhone >

Move Data from Android >

Don't Transfer Apps & Data >

Log in with Apple ID

Type your Apple ID & login code in the appropriate fields, or touch the **"Forgot your password or don't have an Apple ID?"** option to create a new Apple ID, setup Apple ID later, or recover your password or Apple ID.

If you have multiple Apple IDs, touch the **"Use a different Apple ID for iTunes & iCloud?"** option

After signing in with your Apple ID, you may be asked for a verification code from your old device.

Enable automatic updates & setup other features

Adhere to the directives on your screen to allow your iPhone operating system to automatically update and setup other features such as Location Services, Face-Time, Analytics & iMessage.

Setup Siri & other services

You will be prompted to setup or activate features & services, like

If you're logged in with your Apple ID, adhere to the directives on your screen to setup Apple Pay & iCloud Keychain.

Setup Screen Time & other display options

Adhere to the directives on your screen to setup Screen-Time, which provides you an idea of the amount of time you spend on your iPhone. It also allows you to set a time limit for using applications each day.

You can also activate True Tone, and utilize Display Zoom to change the text & icon size on your screen.

BASIC SETTINGS

Wake your phone

When your phone screen turns off, follow the directions below to wake it:

❖ Press the Side button.

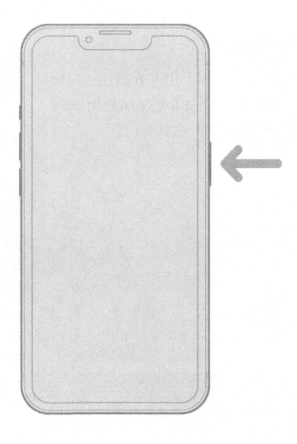

❖ Raise your phone.

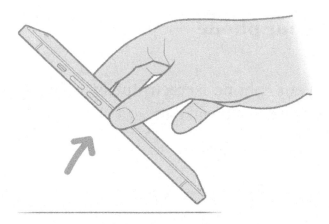

Note: To disable this feature, enter the Settings application> Display & brightness.

❖ Tap your iPhone screen.

Basic gestures

Use the following gestures to interact with your iPhone.

Long-press. Touch & hold an item in an application or in the Controls Centre to preview its content & perform quick actions.

Swipe. Move one of your fingers across your display quickly.

Scroll. Move one of your fingers across your display without lifting. For instance, in the Photos application, you can scroll up or down to check out more pictures. Swipe to scroll faster; tap your display to stop scrolling.

Zoom. Pinch open on your screen to zoom in. Pinch closed to zoom out.

You can also double-tap an image, a web page, or a map in the Maps application to zoom in, and tap it twice again to zoom out.

Go to the Home Screen. Swipe up from the lower edge of your display to go back to the Home screen from any app.

Control Center. Swipe down from the upper right edge of your screen to reveal the Controls Center. long-press any of the controls to see more options. You can add or remove controls, in the Settings application> Control Center.

Application switcher. Swipe up from the lower edge of your screen, and then stop in the middle of your display. Swipe right to view the open applications, then touch the application you want to make use of.

Use Apple Pay. Press the side button two times to reveal your Apple Pay default card, then stare at your screen to authenticate with Face ID.

Use Accessibility Shortcut. Press the Side button thee times.

Use Emergency SOS. Press the side button and any of the volume buttons at the same time until you see the sliders, then slide the Emergency SOS slider.

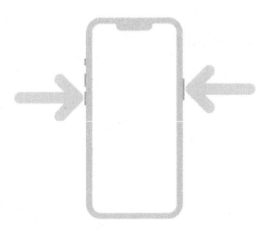

Turn off. Press the side button and any of the volume buttons at the same time until you see the sliders, then slide the Power off slider. Or enter the Settings application, touch General, then touch Shut Down.

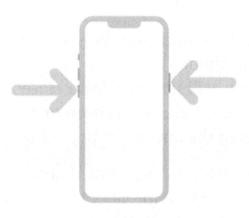

Force restart. Press & release the Increase volume button, press & release the Decrease volume button, and then long-press the Side button until you see the Apple logo.

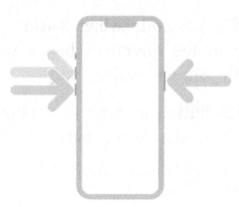

Unlock your iPhone with Face ID

If you activated Face ID when setting up your phone, adhere to the directives below to unlock your device with Face ID.

* Press the side button to wake your phone, then stare at your phone
  The lock icon will animate from closed to open to show that your phone has been unlocked.
* Swipe up from the lower part of your display.

Press the side button to lock your iPhone. If you do not touch your screen for about a minute, your phone will automatically lock.

Unlock iPhone with passcode

If you created a passcode when setting up your phone, adhere to the directives below to unlock your device with your passcode.

* Press the side button to wake your phone, then Swipe up from the lower part of your lock screen.
* Insert your passcode

Press the side button to lock your iPhone. If you do not touch your screen for about a minute, your phone will automatically lock.

Find Settings on your phone

You can find the settings you want to change in the Settings application.

❖ Touch the Settings application's icon  in the Application Library or on your Home Screen.

Swipe down from the upper part of your screen to bring the search bar out, then type a word—"iCloud," for instance—then touch any of the settings.

Set up an eSIM

Your iPhone can store an eSIM provided by your carrier. If your SIM carrier allows eSIM Carrier Activation or eSIM Quick Transfer, you can turn on your new phone and adhere to the guidelines to activate your eSIM during setup.

If you've already setup your device, you can carry out any of the below:

❖ Activation of eSIM Carrier: Some carriers can assign a new eSIM to you; contact your SiM carrier to begin the process. When you get the "Complete Cellular Setup" notification, touch it. Or enter the Settings application> Cellular, and then touch the **Setup Cellular** button or the **Add eSIM** button.
❖ Quick eSIM Transfer: Some SIM carriers allow users to transfer a phone number from their old phone to their new phone without contacting

them. Ensure you are logged in with your Apple ID on the two devices or make sure your old iPhone is unlocked, close to your new phone with Bluetooth activated, and is using iOS 16.

On your new phone, enter the Settings application> Cellular, touch the **Add eSIM** button or the **Setup Cellular** button, then touch **Transfer From Nearby Phone** or select a phone number. Adhere to the directives on your old phone to confirm the transfer.

❖ Scan the QR code sent by your SIM carrier: Enter the Settings application> Cellular, touch the **Add eSIM** button or the **Setup Cellular** button, then touch the **Use QR Code** button. (You may have to touch Other Options first.) Set your phone in a way that the QR code can be seen in the frame on your screen, or insert the information manually. You might be prompted to type a verification code sent to you by your SIM carrier.

❖ Port from another phone: If your old device is an iPhone, contact your carrier to transfer your number.

❖ Activate service from your SIM carrier's application: Enter the Application Store, download your SIM carrier's application, and then activate mobile service in the application.

Install a physical SIM

❖ Put a SIM ejecting tool in the small hole of the SIM plate, then push it inside the hole to bring the tray out.

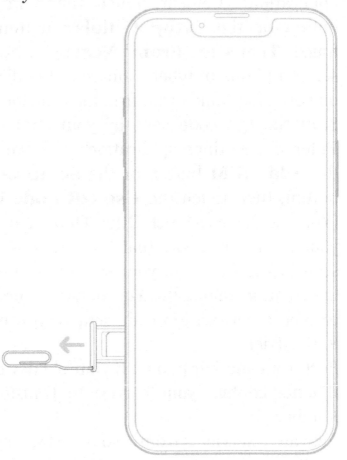

❖ Bring the tray out of your phone.
❖ Put your SIM card on the plate.

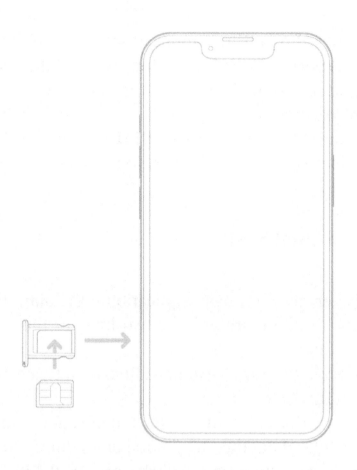

- ❖ Put the SIM plate inside your phone.
- ❖ If your SIM card has a pin, enter the PIN correctly when asked to.

Convert a Physical SIM to an eSIM

If your carrier supports it, adhere to the directives below to convert your physical SIM to an eSIM.

❖ Enter the Settings application> Cellular, touch the **Setup Cellular** button or the **Add eSIM** button, and then pick the number with a physical SIM.
❖ Touch the **Convert to eSIM** button, and then adhere to the directives on your screen.

Setup Dual SIM

❖ Enter the Settings application> Cellular, then ensure there are at least two lines in the SIMS section.
❖ Enable two lines — touch a line, then touch Turn On this Line.
❖ Select the standard line for mobile data — touch Cellular data, then touch one of the lines. To use the two lines depending on availability & coverage, activate Allow Cellular Data Switching.
❖ Select a standard line for calls—touch the **Default Voice Line** button, then touch one of the lines.

Connect your phone to the Internet using a WiFi network

❖ Enter the Settings application> WiFi, and then activate WiFi.
❖ Touch any of the below:
   ➢ A Network: Insert the password, if necessary.
   ➢ Others: To join a hidden network, type the network's name, security type, & password.

If you see the Wi-Fi icon 📶 at the upper part of your display, it means that your phone has connected to a WiFi network. (To confirm this, enter the Safari application and visit a webpage.) When you return to the same location, your phone will reconnect to the WiFi network.

Join a Personal Hotspot

If another iPhone or an iPad is sharing their Personal Hotspot, you can use its mobile Internet connection.

❖ Enter the Settings application> WiFi, then select the device that's sharing the Personal Hotspot.
❖ When asked to enter a password, type the passcode displayed in the Settings application > Cellular > Personal Hotspot on the iPhone or iPad that's sharing the Personal Hotspot.

Connect your phone to the internet using a Cellular network

❖ Make sure your SIM and is activated & unlocked.
❖ Enter the Settings application> Cellular.
❖ Make sure Cellular data is activated. If you are making use of two SIM cards, touch Cellular Data, then check the line selected.

Manage Apple ID settings on iPhone

The account you use to gain access to Apple services (like iCloud, Face-Time, Application Store, etc.) is known as your Apple ID.

Sign in with your Apple ID

❖ Enter the Settings application.
❖ Touch **Sign in to iPhone**.
❖ Type your Apple ID & password in the appropriate fields
You can create an Apple ID if you do not have one

❖ If your account is protected with 2-factor authentication, insert the 6-digit code for verification.

Change your Apple ID settings

❖ Enter the Settings application> [your name].
❖ Carry out any of the below:
  ➢ Update your profile
  ➢ Check out & manage your subscriptions
  ➢ Manage family sharing
  ➢ Add or delete account recovery contacts
  ➢ change your passcode
  ➢ Update your payment method

Activate Low Power Mode

The Low Power Mode feature minimizes the amount of power your phone makes use of when the battery is low. It improves performance for important tasks such as making & calls; sending messages & e-mails; Internet access; and others.

Carry out one of the below to enable or disable Low Power Mode:

❖ In the Settings application: Enter the Settings application> Battery.
❖ In the Controls Centre: Enter the Settings application> Controls Center, then select Low power mode and add it to the Controls Centre.

Optimize your phone battery charging

Your phone has a feature that slows the battery's aging rate by reducing the time it takes to fully charge. This feature makes use of machine learning to understand your daily charging patterns, after understanding it, your iPhone will not charge past 80 percent until when it's close to when you need it.

❖ Enter the Settings application> Battery, and then touch Battery Health.
❖ Activate Optimized Battery Charging.

Check the health of your iPhone battery

❖ Enter the Settings application and touch Battery.
❖ Touch Battery Health.
  Your phone will display info about your battery's capacity, peak performance, and when your battery needs to be serviced.

See battery usage information

Enter the Settings application> Battery.

Adjust the volume on your Phone

When listening to music, videos, or other media on your phone, you can use the buttons on the left side of your phone to change the volume.

Change the volume level in the Control Center

You can adjust the volume level in the Controls Centre.

Swipe down from the upper right corner of your display to reveal the Controls Center, and then slide the volume slider .

Put your iPhone in silent mode

Use Ring mode   Use Silent mode

To put your phone in silent mode, move the Silent/Ring switch (when you see an orange colour on the switch it means your phone has entered silent mode). Move the switch back to turn off silent mode.

The front of the iPhone has a Ring/Silent switch on the left side, above the volume buttons.

Open applications on your phone

You can launch apps from the Home screen or the Application Library.

❖ To enter the Home screen, swipe up from the lower edge of your display.

❖ Swipe to the left to view applications on other pages of the Home Screen.

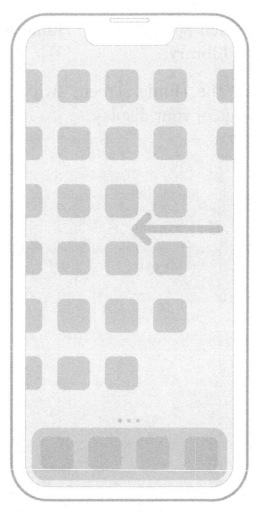

❖ Touch the icon of an application to launch it.
❖ To go back to the Home screen, swipe up from the lower edge of your display.

Find applications in the Application Library

The Application Library displays your applications sorted into categories like Entertainment, Utilities, & Social. The applications you use more often are at the top of your screen and the top of their categories, so you can easily find & launch them.

To find & open an application in your Application Library, adhere to the directives below:

❖ To get to the Application Library from your Home Screen, swipe left till you pass all the Home screen pages.
❖ Touch the search bar at the upper part of your display, then type the name of the application you want. Or scroll down to view the list.
❖ Touch an application to launch it.

Hide & display Home Screen pages

Since all your applications are in the Application Library, you may not need a lot of Home Screen pages for applications. You can hide some pages, which will bring the Application Library closer to the first page of your Home screen.

❖ Long-press the Home Screen till the applications start vibrating.
❖ Touch the dots at the lower part of your display. Next, you will see thumbnail pictures of your Home Screen pages with checkmarks under them.

❖ To hide the Home screen pages, touch to remove the check marks
Touch to add the checkmark to show the Home Screen pages you've hidden.

❖ Touch the Done button two times.

Rearrange the Home Screen pages

If the home screen has many pages, you can rearrange them. For instance, you can put your favourite applications on one Home Screen page, and then make that page your first Home Screen page.

❖ Long-press the Home Screen till the applications start vibrating.

❖ Touch the dots at the lower part of your display. Next, you will see thumbnail pictures of your Home Screen pages with checkmarks under them.

❖ To move a page, long press its thumbnail image, and then drag it to another location.
❖ Touch the Done button twice

Change where new applications get downloaded

After downloading new applications from the Application Store, you can add them to your Home screen and the Application Library, or just the Application Library.

❖ Enter the Settings application> Home Screen.
❖ Select whether to add new applications to the Home Screen and the Application Library, or just the Application Library.

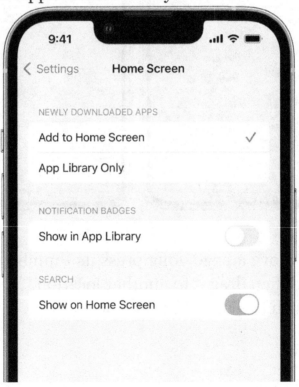

Application Switcher

Open the Application Switcher to quickly switch between open applications on your phone.

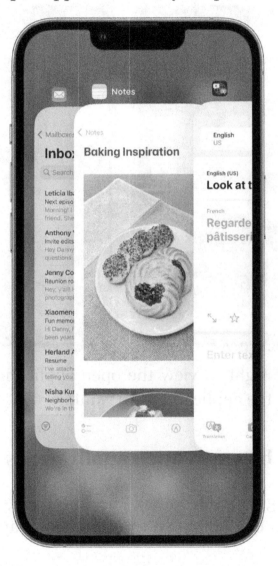

❖ To see all open applications in the Application Switcher, Swipe up from the lower edge of your screen, and then stop in the middle of your display.

❖ Swipe right to view the open applications, then touch the application you want.

Switch between open applications

Swipe right or left along the lower edge of your screen to quickly move from one open application to another.

Quit an application

To quit an application, open the Application Switcher, swipe to the application, then swipe up on it.

Dictate text

You can dictate text anywhere you can type on your phone.

Enable Dictation

❖ Enter the Settings application, touch General, then touch Keyboard.

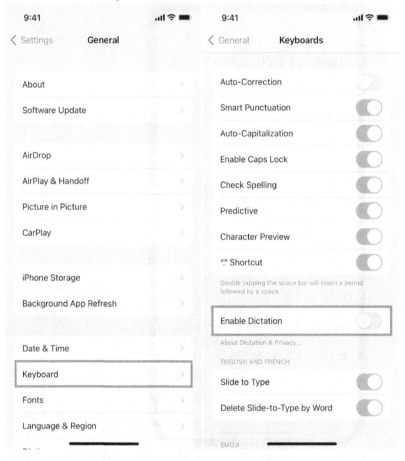

❖ Activate **Enable Dictation**.

Dictate

❖ Touch where you want to inset text.

❖ Touch the Dictate icon 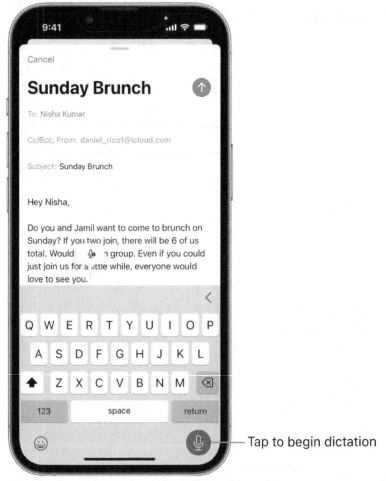 on your keyboard, then say what you want.

Tap to begin dictation

As you speak, your phone will automatically insert punctuation marks for you.

Note: You can disable this feature in Settings application> General > Keyboards and then deactivate Auto-Punctuation.

❖ When you're done, touch the Stop Dictation icon .

Select & edit text

In applications on your phone, you can use your keyboard to select and edit text.

❖ To highlight/select text, carry out any of the below:
  • Use one of your fingers to tap a word twice quickly to highlight it.
  • Use one of your fingers to tap a word in a paragraph three times to select the paragraph.
  • Highlight a text block: Double-tap & hold the 1st word in the text block, then drag to the last word.
❖ Once you've selected the text you want, you can type or select any of the editing options:
  ➢ Cut: Touch the **Cut** button or pinched closed with 3 of your fingers twice.

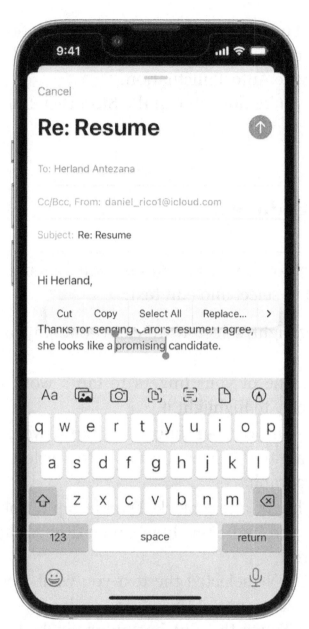

> Copy: Touch the **Copy** button or pinch closed with 3 of your fingers.

- ➤ Paste: Touch the button or pinch open with 3 of your fingers.
- ➤ Select All: Highlight all text in the file.
- ➤ Replace: See recommended replacement text.
- ➤ Format: Format the text you've highlighted.
- ➤ 〉: See other options.

Text replacement

Create text replacements that you can use to insert words or phrases by typing just a few letters. For instance, write "omw" to insert "On my way" Type "omv" to enter. It's already created for you, but you can add your own.

Adhere to the directives below to create text replacements.

- ❖ While typing in the text field, long-press the Emoji key ☺ or the Keyboard key ⊕.
- ❖ Touch Keyboards Settings, then touch the **Text Replacements** button.
- ❖ Touch the Add icon at the upper right of your screen.
- ❖ Write a phrase in the Phrases field, and write the shortcut in the Shortcut field.

Add or remove a keyboard for another language

❖ Enter the Settings application, touch General, then touch Keyboard.

❖ Touch Keyboard, then carry out any of the below:
  ➢ Add keyboard: Touch the **Add a New Keyboard** button, then select a keyboard from the list.
  ➢ Remove a keyboard: Touch the **Edit** button, touch the **Remove** icon beside the keyboard you plan to remove, touch the **Delete** button, and then touch Done.
  ➢ Rearrange the keyboard list: Touch the **Edit** button, drag the Edit icon beside the Keyboard to a new location in the list, then touch the Done button.

Switch to another keyboard

❖ While typing in the text field, long-press the Emoji key or the Keyboard key .
❖ Touch the keyboard you want to switch to.

Multitask on iPhone

You can use Face-Time or watch videos while using other applications.

While watching a video, touch the Picture icon .

The video window shrinks to the corner of the display to reveal the Home screen. With the video window showing, you can carry out any of the below:

* Change the size of the vide window: Pinch open on the window to make it bigger. Pinch closed to make the window smaller.
* Touch the window to hide or display controls.
* Move the video window by dragging it to another corner of your display.
* Hide the video window by dragging it off the right or left edge of your display.
* Touch the Close icon to close the video window.
* Touch the Full Screen icon in the window to go back to a full-screen window.

Access features from the Lock screen

The Lock Screen appears when you turn on or wake your phone. You can access useful features & info from the Lock Screen, even when your phone is locked.

From the lock screen, carry out any of the below:

- ❖ Open the camera: Swipe left.
- ❖ Open the Controls Centre: Swipe down from the upper right edge of your screen
- ❖ See notifications: swipe up from the middle of your screen
- ❖ View widgets: Swipe to the right.

Dynamic Island

You can check notifications & activities in progress, such as music playing, AirDrop connections, and Maps directions, in the Dynamic Island.

A Voice Memos recording showing in the Dynamic Island

Long press the Dynamic Island to make it bigger so that you can get more information about an activity.

Perform quick actions from the Home Screen and Application Library

Long press an application on your Home screen or Application Library to open the quick actions menu.

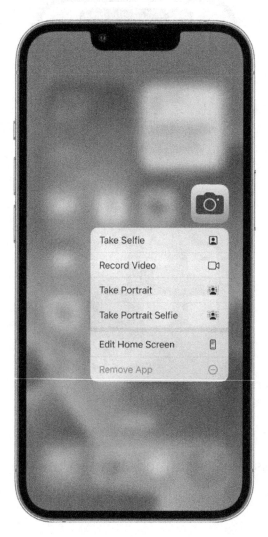

For instance:

❖ Long-press the Camera app icon 📷 , then select Record Video.

❖ Long-press the Maps app icon 🧭 , then select Send Location.

❖ Long-press the Notes app icon 📝 , then select New Note.

Search on your iPhone

You can search for contacts & applications, and contents in applications like Photos, Messages, & Mail. You can also check stock and currency data and perform calculations.

Select which applications to include in the Search

❖ Enter the Settings application, touch Siri & Search.
❖ Scroll, touch an application, then activate or deactivate **Show Application in Search**.

Search with your phone

❖ Tap the Spotlight icon in the lower part of your Home screen or swipe down on the Lock screen.

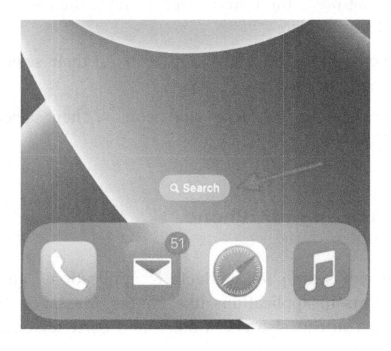

❖ Type what you want in the search bar.
❖ Carry out any of the below:
  ➢ Touch the Search button to see more results on your display.
  ➢ Touch a suggested application to launch it.
  ➢ Touch a suggested site to visit it.
  ➢ Start a new search: Touch the Clear icon ⊗ in the search bar.

AirDrop

AirDrop allows you to send pictures, videos, sites, locations, & more wirelessly to nearby Mac computers & other Apple devices (requires iOS 7, iPadOS 13, macOS X 10.10 or after). AirDrop sends data via WiFi & Bluetooth - both must be enabled.

Send something using AirDrop

❖ Open the item, then touch the Share icon⬆, Share, AirDrop, the More Options icon•••, or any other icon that shows the application's sharing options.

❖ Touch the AirDrop icon◉ in the sharing options row, then touch the nearby AirDrop user's profile photo.

If the person does not appear as an AirDrop user, tell the person to open the Controls Centre on their iPod touch, iPad, or iPhone and let AirDrop receive items. If you want to send an item to a Mac user, tell the person to allow themselves to be discovered in AirDrop in the Finder.

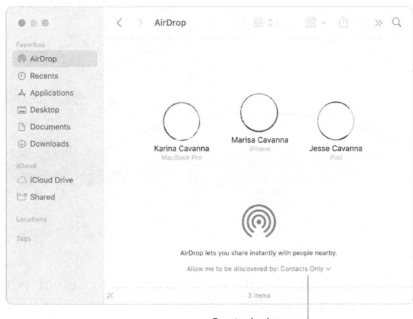

Control who can
send items to you.

Let others send things to your iPhone via AirDrop

❖ Swipe down from the upper right edge of your screen to reveal the Controls Center, long press the upper left set of controls, then touch the AirDrop icon .

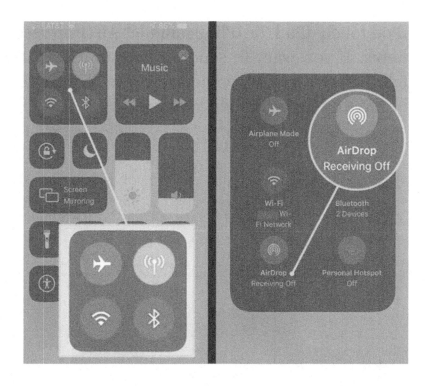

❖ Tap Contacts Only or Everybody to select who you want to get items from.

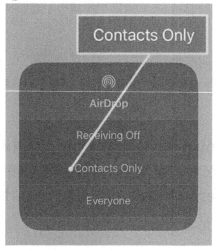

You can accept or reject the request as they arrive.

Take a screenshot

You can take a picture of your screen and share it with others or use it in a document.

❖ Press the side button and any of the volume buttons at the same time.

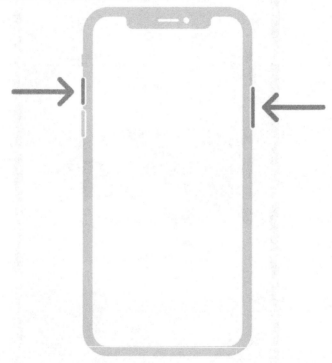

❖ Touch the screenshot in the bottom left part of your screen, then touch the **Done** button.
❖ Select Save To Files, Save to Photo, or Delete Screenshots.

If you picked the **Save to Photos** option, you can find it in the Screenshots folder in the Photos application, or in the All Photos folder if iCloud Photos is enabled in the Settings application> Photos.

Save a full-page screenshot in PDF format

You can capture a full page, scrolling screen shot of a webpage, doc, or e-mail that is longer than the length of your phone screen, then save it in PDF format.

❖ Press the side button and any of the volume buttons at the same time.
❖ Touch the screenshot in the bottom left part of your screen, then touch the **Full Page** button.
❖ Carry out any of the below:
  ➢ Save the screenshot: Touch the **Done** button, select Save PDF to Files, select a location, and then touch the **Save** button.
  ➢ Share the file: Touch the Share icon , select a sharing option (for instance, Mail, Messages, or AirDrop), type any other needed info, then send the PDF file.

Record your screen

You can record your screen and capture the audio as well.

❖ Enter the Settings application> Controls Centre

❖ Touch the Add icon beside Screen Recording.

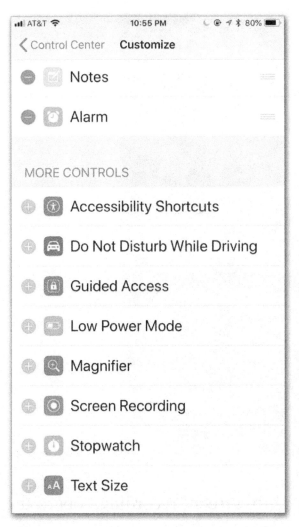

❖ Swipe down from the upper right edge of your screen to reveal the Controls Center, then touch the Screen Recording icon.

Your phone will start recording its screen after 3 seconds

❖ To stop screen recording, open the Controls Centre, touch the Stop Recording icon  or touch the red status bar at the upper part of your display, and then touch the Stop button.

Enter the Photos application, then select your recording.

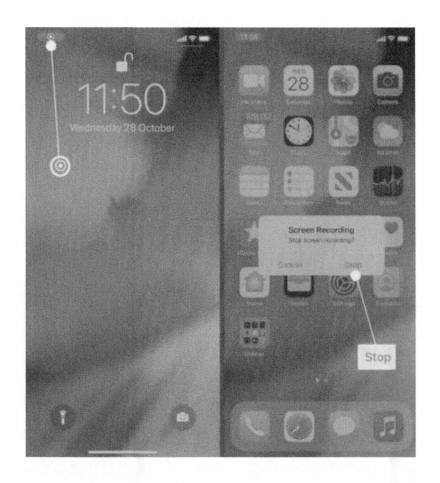

iCloud

iCloud saves your pictures, movies, docs, backups, and more automatically. iCloud also gives you an e-mail account & 5GB of free storage space

Change iCloud settings

❖ Enter the Settings application, touch [your name], then touch iCloud.

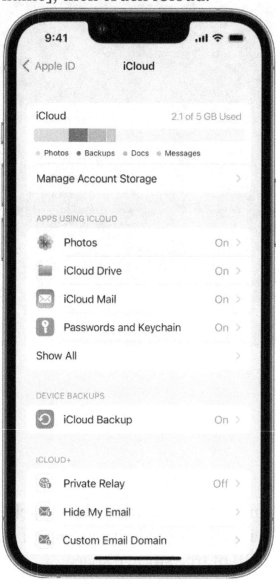

❖ Carry out any of the below:
  ➢ Check the status of your iCloud storage.
  ➢ Activate features you want to make use of, like iCloud Back Up, Photos, etc.

Upgrade, cancel, or change your iCloud+ subscription

❖ Enter the Settings application, touch [your name], then touch iCloud.
❖ Touch the **Manage Accounts Storage** button, touch the **Change Storage Plans** button, choose an option, and then adhere to the directives on your display.

CUSTOMIZE YOUR PHONE

Change your phone sounds & vibrations

Change the sound your phone plays when you receive an email, text, voicemail, call, reminder, or other notification in the Settings app.

❖ Enter the Settings application, and touch Sound & Haptics.
❖ Move the slider in the Ringtone & Alert Volume section to adjust the volume of all sounds.
❖ Touch a sound type, like new mail or ringing tone, to set the tone & vibration pattern for the sound.
❖ Carry out any of the below:
  ➢ Select a sound (scroll to view all).
    Ringing tones play for calls, alarms, and clock timers; Text tones are for new voicemail, text messages, and other alerts.
  ➢ Touch Vibration, then select a vibration type, or touch the **Create New Vibration** button to create one for yourself.

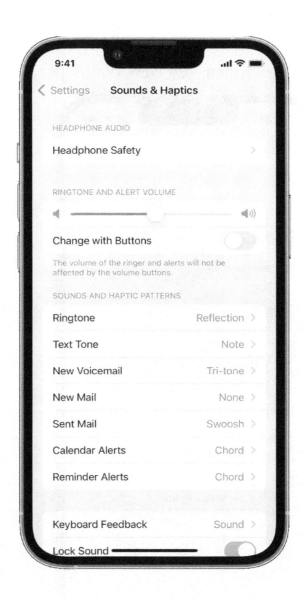

Change the wallpaper on your phone

You can change the Lock Screen and Home Screen wallpaper on your phone.

❖ Enter the Settings application, touch Wallpaper, and then touch Add New Wallpaper.

The wallpaper gallery will appear.

❖ Carry out any of the below:

    ➢ Touch any of the buttons at the upper part of
       the wallpaper gallery (Photos Shuffle, People,

Photo, etc.) to design your wallpaper with a picture, an emoji pattern, etc.

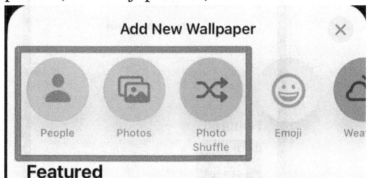

> Touch one of the wallpapers in any of the categories (Photo Shuffle, Suggested Photos, or Featured).

❖ Touch the **Add** button, then carry out any of the below:

> Touch the **Set as Wallpaper Pair** button to choose whether to use the wallpaper on your Lock Screen & Home Screen.

> To make additional changes to the Home Screen, touch the **Customize Home Screen** button. Touch a colour to change the colour of the wallpaper, touch the Photos icon to use a custom picture, or choose Blur to blur the wallpaper.

Adjust the screen brightness manually

To make the phone screen brighter or dimmer, carry out any of the below:

❖ Swipe down from the upper right edge of your screen to reveal the Controls Center, and then drag the Brightness switch ☀.

❖ Enter the Settings application> Display & Brightness, and then slide the slider.

Adjust screen brightness automatically

Your iPhone can use its inbuilt ambient light sensor to adjust the screen's brightness to fit the current lighting conditions.

❖ Enter the Settings application, and touch Accessibility.
❖ Touch Display & Text Size, then activate Auto-Brightness.

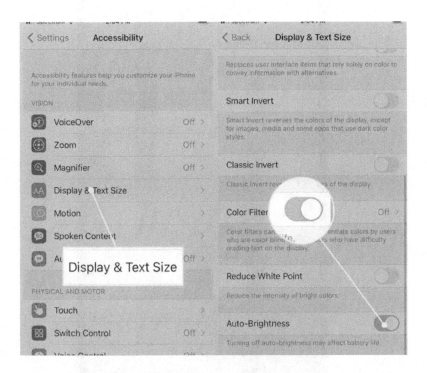

Enable or disable Dark Mode

Dark Mode gives your phone a dark colour scheme that is perfect for low-light environments.

Carry out any of the below:

❖ Swipe down from the upper right edge of your screen to reveal the Controls Center, long press the Brightness button ☀, then touch the Dark Mode icon ◑ to activate or deactivate Dark Mode.

❖ Enter the Settings application, touch Display & Brightness, then touch Dark to activate Dark Mode or choose Light to deactivate it.

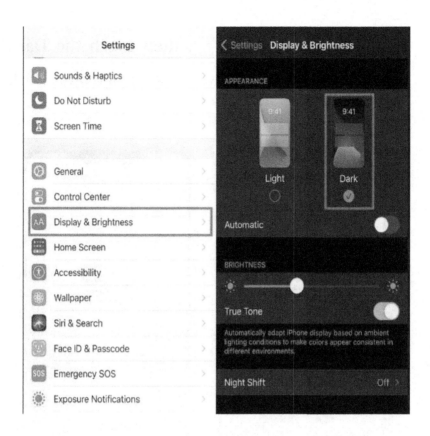

Set dark mode to activate or deactivate automatically

You can programme Dark Mode to activate at specific times in the Settings application.

❖ Enter the Settings application, touch Display & Brightness.
❖ Activate Automatic, then touch Options.

Page | 90

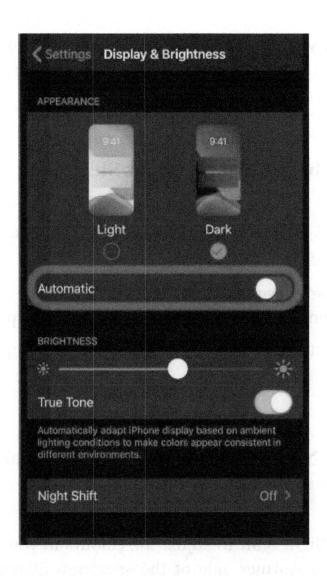

❖ Choose Custom Schedule or Sunset to Sunrise.
  If you picked Custom Schedule, touch the
  options to choose when you want Dark Mode to
  activate or deactivate.

If you choose **Sunset to Sunrise**, your phone will use the data from your clock and geo-location to know when it's nighttime for you.

Enable or disable Night Shift

Night Shift is helpful when you are in a dark room during daytime.

Swipe down from the upper right edge of your screen to reveal the Controls Center, long press the Brightness button ☀ , then touch the Night Shift icon ☾

Set Night Shift to activate or deactivate automatically

Set Night Shift to adjust the colours in your screen to the warmer side of the spectrum at night and make it easier to look at your screen.

❖ Enter the Settings application, touch Display & Brightness, then touch Night mode.
❖ Activate Scheduled.

❖ To change the colour balance for Night Shift, slide the slider in the Colour Temperature section to the cooler or warmer end of the spectrum.

❖ Touch From, then Choose Custom Schedule or Sunset to Sunrise.

If you picked Custom Schedule, touch the options to choose when you want Night Shift to activate or deactivate.

If you choose **Sunset to Sunrise**, your phone will use the data from your clock and geo-location to know when it's nighttime for you.

Activate or deactivate True Tone

True Tone adjusts the colour & intensity of your screen to match the ambient light.

Carry out any of the below:

❖ Swipe down from the upper right edge of your screen to reveal the Controls Center, long press the Brightness button ☀ , then touch the True Tone icon ☀ to activate or deactivate True Tone

❖ Enter the Settings application> Display & Brightness, then activate or deactivate True Tone

Keep your phone display on longer

Your phone display goes dark & locks when it's not being used. If you want the screen to stay on longer, you can change how long it takes your device to automatically dim & lock.

Enter the Settings application> Display and Brightness > Auto-lock, then select the time length.

Keep your Lock Screen visible

The Always On feature allows a dark version of the Lock Screen to remain visible even when your phone is locked, so you can look at the Lock Screen to view important information, like time, date, alerts, etc.

The display will automatically turn off when your phone is face down

The Always On feature is enabled by default. To deactivate it, enter the Settings application> Display and brightness, then deactivate Always On.

Magnify your phone screen

You can see bigger controls on your screen.

* Enter the Settings application> Display and Brightness > Displays Zoom.
* Choose Larger Text to make all text on your phone bigger.
* Touch Done, then touch Use Zoomed.

Change the language & region of your phone

* Enter the Settings application, and touch General > Language & Region.
* Set any of the below:
  * Language for your phone
  * Region
  * Calendar format
  * Temperature unit (Fahrenheit or Celsius)
  * Measurement system
  * First day of the week

> Live text (selectable text in pictures to copy or take action on)
❖ To add another keyboard & language to your phone, touch the **Add Language** button, then choose a language.

Change the time & date on your phone

By default, the time & date displayed on the Lock screen is automatically adjusted based on your location. But you can change then if you want.

❖ Enter the Settings application> General > Date and Time.
❖ Activate any of the below:
> Set automatically: Your phone will automatically set the time & date using the network.

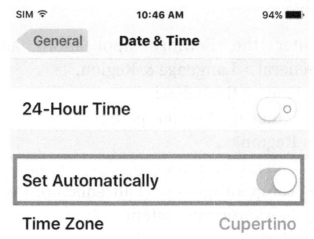

> ➤ 24-hour Time: Your phone will show the hours from 0 to 23.

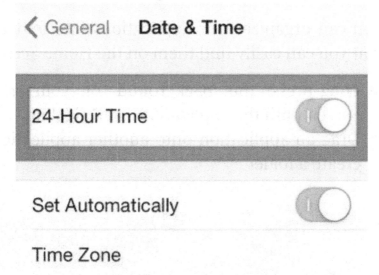

To change the specified time & date, deactivate Set Automatically, then change the date & time

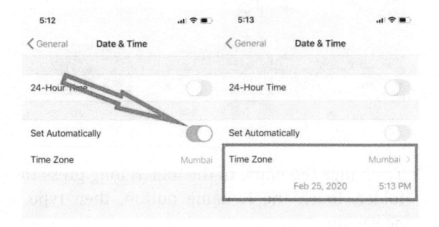

Organize your applications in folders

You can organize your applications into folders so that you can easily find them on the Home Screen.

❖ Long-press the background of your Home Screen until the applications start jiggling.
❖ Drag an application onto another application to create a folder.

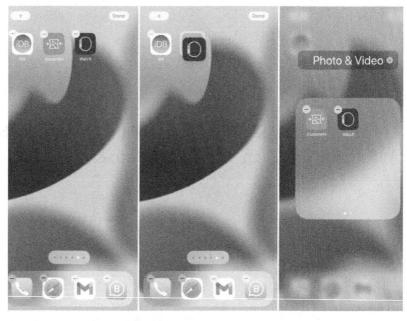

❖ To change the name of the folder, long press the folder, touch the Rename button, then type a new name.

❖ When you are done, touch the Done button, then touch the background of your Home Screen two times.

To delete a folder, open the folder, then drag all the applications out of the folder. The folder will be deleted automatically.

Move applications on your iPhone's Home screen

You can change your Home Screen's layout by moving applications from one Home Screen page to another.

❖ Long-press an application on your Home Screen, then touch the **Edit Home Screen** button.
  The applications will start jiggling.
❖ Drag the application to any of the following locations:
  ➢ Other places on the page
  ➢ Another Home Screen page
    Drag the application to the right edge of your display. You may have to wait for a few seconds for the next page to show.

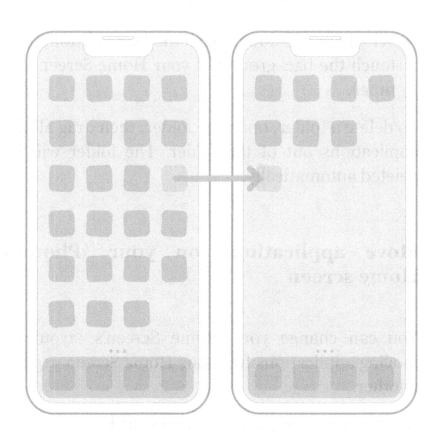

❖ When you're done, tap the Done button.

Reset your Home Screen and applications to their original format

❖ Enter the Settings application, touch General > Transfer, or reset iPhone.

❖ Touch the **Reset** button, touch the **Reset Home screen layout** button, and then touch the **Reset Home Screen** button.

Any folders you have created will be removed, and the applications you have downloaded will be sorted alphabetically after the applications that came with your phone.

Remove applications from your phone

❖ Remove an application from your Home Screen: Long-press the application on your Home screen, touch the **Remove App** button, then touch the **Remove from Home Screen** button to leave the application in the Application Library, or touch the **Delete App** button to remove the application from your phone.
❖ Delete an application from the Application library & Home screen: Long-press the application in the Application Library, touch the **Delete Application** button and then touch the **Delete** button

Use and customize the Control Center on your device

The Controls Centre on your phone provides quick access to useful controls like airplane mode, DND, screen brightness, and applications.

To reveal the Controls Center, swipe down from the upper right corner of your screen. Swipe up from the lower part of your screen to close the Controls Centre.

Access more controls in the Control Center

Most controls have more options. Long press a control to check out the available options. For instance, in Control Center, you can:

❖ Long-press the upper left set of controls, then touch the AirDrop icon to see the AirDrop options.

❖ Long-press the Camera icon to take a selfie, record a video, etc.

Touch and hold to see Camera options.

Add & organize controls

You can personalize the Controls Centre by adding more controls and shortcuts to a lot of applications, like Calculator, Notes, etc.

❖ Enter the Settings application, and touch Control Center.

❖ To add or remove a control, touch the Add icon ⊕ or the Remove icon ⊖ beside a control.

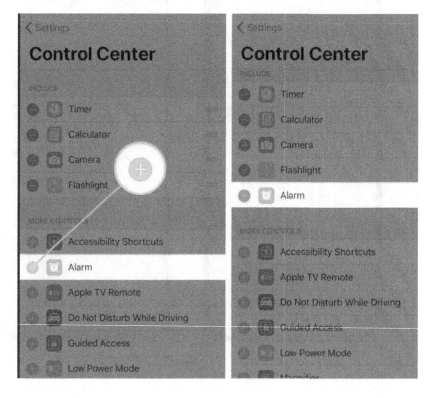

❖ To change the position of a control, touch the Edit icon ☰ beside the control and then drag it to another location.

Change or lock the screen orientation on your phone

Most applications have a different look when your iPhone is rotated.

You can lock your phone's screen orientation so that it does not change when you turn your phone.

Swipe down from the upper right corner of your screen to open the Controls Center, and then touch the Orientation Lock icon .

When the screen orientation is locked, you will see the Orientation Lock icon in the status bar

Use the calculator

Perform basic arithmetic calculations in the Calculator application

Use the scientific calculator

Turn your phone to landscape orientation

Copy, or erase numbers

❖ Copy calculation results: Long-press the result on your screen, touch the **Copy** button, then paste the somewhere else.
❖ Swipe to the left or right to erase the last digit.
❖ Clear the screen: Touch the (C) key to clear the last entry or touch the (AC) key to erase all entries.

Check the time in cities around the world

Use the Clock application to find the local time in different parts of the world.

❖ In the Clock application, touch World Clock.
❖ To manage your cities list, touch the **Edit** button
and then carry out any of the below:

> To add cities: Touch the Add icon , and then select a city.
> Delete cities: Touch the Delete icon ⊖.

Set an alarm

❖ In the Clock application, touch the **Alarm** button, then touch the Add icon ✛.
❖ Set the alarm, then select any of the options below:
  > Repeat: Select the week days
  > Label: Name the alarm.
  > Sound: Select a ringing tone, song, or vibration.
  > Snooze: Give yourself some time to rest.
❖ Touch the Save button.

To make changes to the alarm, touch the **Edit** button at the upper left of your screen, and then touch the alarm time.

Turn off a regular alarm

Touch the button beside the alarm time.

Remove an alarm

In the Clock application, touch the Edit button at the upper left part of your display, touch the Delete icon⬤, then touch the **Delete button**.

Keep track of time with the stopwatch

* In the Clock application, touch Stopwatch. Swipe the stopwatch to move from digital face to analog face.
* Touch the Start button. The timer will continue even if you enter another application.
* Touch the **Lap** button to record a split or lap.
* Touch the Stop button to finish recording.
* Touch the Reset button to reset the clock.

Create Memoji

You can create your Memoji - pick skin color, glasses, headwear, etc. You can design many Memojis for different moods.

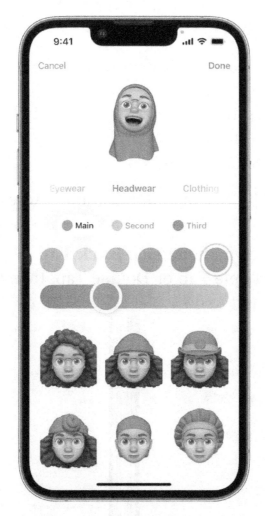

❖ In a conversation in the Messages application, touch the Memoji icon 🐵, and then touch the New Memoji icon ✚.

❖ Touch the features & options you want.

❖ Touch the **Done** button to add the Memoji to your collection.

Tap the back of your phone to perform actions

You can tap the back of your phone twice or three times to perform actions like, taking screenshots, running a shortcut, etc.

❖ Enter the Settings application> Accessibility > Touch
❖ Scroll down, then touch **Back Tap**
❖ Touch Triple Tap or Double Tap, then pick what you want it to do

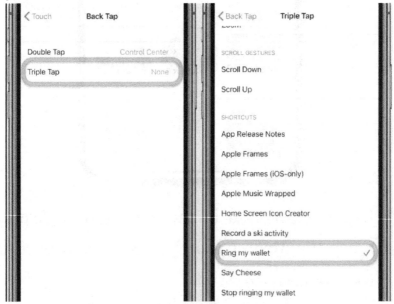

❖ Tap the back of your phone two times or three times quickly to perform the action you've programmed.

PERSONALIZE YOUR LOCK SCREEN

You can customize the Lock Screen by adding wallpaper, personalizing the fonts & colours, etc. You can also add widgets with info from your favourite applications to your Lock Screen, like the weather, calendar events, etc.

You can create multiple Lock Screens & switch between them easily. Because each Lock Screen can be linked to Focus, you can switch to a different Lock Screen and change your focus.

Create a custom Lock Screen

❖ Long-press the Lock Screen until you see the Customize option at the lower part of your display.

If the Customize option does not show up, Long-press the Lock screen again, then insert your login code.

❖ Touch the Add icon  at the lower part of your display.

The Lock Screen wallpaper gallery will appear.

❖ Touch any of the wallpapers to use it as your Lock Screen.

❖ For some types of wallpapers, you can swipe to the right or left to try different colour filters, fonts & patterns.

❖ Touch the **Add** button, then carry out any of the below:
  ➢ Touch the **Set as Wallpaper Pair** button to use the wallpaper on the Lock Screen & Home Screen.
  ➢ Make more changes to your Home Screen: touch the **Customize Home Screen** button. Touch a colour to change the colour of the wallpaper, touch the Gallery icon to make use of a custom picture, or choose Blur to blur the wallpaper.

Add a picture to your Lock Screen

You can select a picture from your Photos library or allow your iPhone to suggest a picture that complements your other Lock Screen settings.

❖ Long-press the Lock Screen until you see the Customize option at the lower part of your display.
  If the Customize option does not show up, Long-press the Lock screen again, then insert your login code.

❖ Touch the Add icon at the lower part of your display, then pick any of the Photos options (Photo Shuffle or Photos) at the upper part of your display

❖ If you select Photos and want to create a multi-layered effect, touch the More Options icon⊙ at the lower part of your display, then select Depth Effect.

❖ To change the position of your selected photo, pinch open on the photo to zoom in on it, drag the photo with 2 of your fingers to move it to the desired position, and then pinch closed to zoom out.

You can also swipe to check out different picture styles that include colour filters & fonts.

❖ If you selected Photos Shuffle, you can browse through the photos by touching the Browse icon ▦ and programme the shuffle frequency by touching the More Options icon⊙, then choosing an option in the Shuffle Frequency section.

Tip: You can add a picture from your Photos library to your Lock Screen & Home Screen. In the Photos application, touch Library, select a picture, and then touch the Share icon⬆. Scroll down and choose **Use as Wallpaper**, touch the **Done** button, then you can choose to display the wallpaper on both the Lock Screen & Home Screen.

Rotate multiple pictures as your Lock Screen wallpaper

❖ Enter the Settings application, and touch Wallpaper.
❖ Touch the **Add a New Wallpaper** button.

❖ Touch the **Photos Shuffle** button from the row of options at the top of your screen.

❖ Set a frequency (Daily, Hourly, Wake Up, or On Tap) on the Photo Shuffle screen. Then select a series of pictures that will change as you use your phone throughout the day.

Photo Shuffle

A dynamic set of photos that shuffle as you use your iPhone throughout the day.

On Tap

On Wake

✓ Hourly

Daily

Shuffle Frequency   Hourly ⌄

Use Featured Photos

Select Photos Manually

❖ Touch the **Done** button

Add widgets to the Lock Screen

Add widgets to your lock screen to get information easily—for instance, calendar events, battery, etc.

❖ Long-press the Lock Screen until you see the Customize option at the lower part of your display.

If the Customize option does not show up, Long-press the Lock screen again, then insert your login code.

❖ Touch the **Customize** button

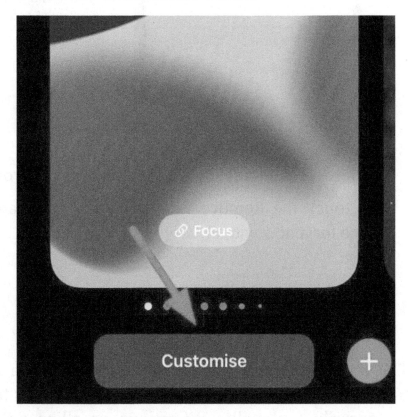

❖ Touch the box under the time to add a widget.

Tap to add widgets to your Lock Screen.

❖ Touch the widgets you want to add.
  If there isn't enough space for new widgets, you
  can touch the Remove Widget icon ⊖ to create
  space for a new widget.

Link a Focus to your Lock Screen

The Focus feature helps you to stay focused on a task by reducing distraction. You can set a Focus to temporarily mute all notifications or allow only certain notifications (for instance, notifications related to the task). When you link a Focus to your

Lock Screen, you can access the Focus features while using that Lock Screen.

❖ Long-press the Lock Screen until you see the Customize option at the lower part of your display.
If the Customize option does not show up, Long-press the Lock screen again, then insert your login code.

❖ Touch the Focus button at the lower part of the wallpaper to view the Focus options, such as DND, Work, Sleep, etc.

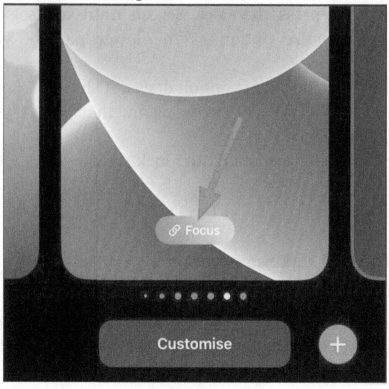

❖ Choose a Focus, and then touch the Close icon
ⓧ .

Switch between Lock Screens

You can create many Lock Screens and move between them throughout the day. If you link a Lock Screen to a particular focus, switching from that lock screen to another will change the Focus.

❖ Long-press the Lock Screen until you see the Customize option at the lower part of your display.
If the Customize option does not show up, Long-press the Lock screen again, then insert your login code.
❖ Swipe to and touch the lock screen you want to use.

Edit a Lock Screen

After creating a custom lock screen, you can adjustments to it.

❖ Long-press the Lock Screen until you see the Customize option at the lower part of your display.
If the Customize option does not show up, Long-press the Lock screen again, then insert your login code.

❖ Swipe to the Lock Screen, then touch the Add icon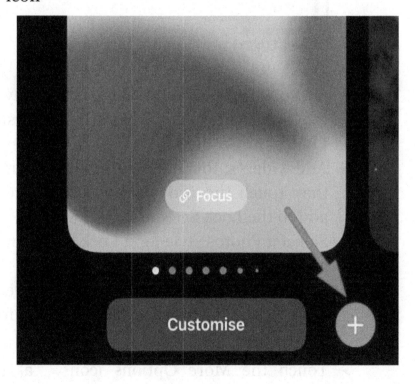

❖ Carry out any of the below:
> Touch any of the buttons at the upper part of the wallpaper gallery (Photos Shuffle,

People, Photo, etc.) to design your wallpaper with a picture, an emoji pattern, etc.

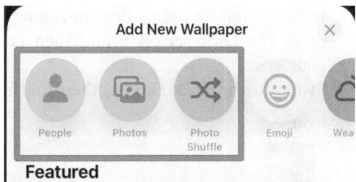

Or, touch one of the wallpapers in any of the categories (Photos Shuffle, Suggested Photos, or Featured).

➢ Add widgets: touch the box under the time, then touch the widgets you would like to add to the Lock Screen.

➢ Select a Photos style for a Lock Screen with a picture: Swipe to make changes to the colour filter (for example, Vivid, Deep, Tone, etc), photo background, and the font for the time.

➢ Touch the More Options icon ⊙ at the lower part of your display, and then select Depth Effect to add a multilayered effect to a Lock Screen (not available in all pictures)

➤ Change the focus: Touch the **Focus** button close to the lower part of the wallpaper, then select a different Focus from the list.
➤ Change the time style: Touch the **Customize** button, touch the time, and then choose a color, shade, & font by touching the Effects icon ●.

Delete a Lock Screen

❖ Long-press the Lock Screen until you see the Customize option at the lower part of your display.
If the Customize option does not show up, Long-press the Lock screen again, then insert your login code.
❖ Swipe to the lock screen you want to erase, swipe up on the Lock screen and then touch the Trash icon 🗑.

CAMERA

This chapter will teach you how to take pictures with your iPhone's camera.

Open the Camera app

Carry out any of the below to open the camera:

❖ Touch the Camera application icon  on your Home Screen.

❖ Press & hold the Camera button  on your iPhone's Lock screen.

❖ Swipe down from the upper right corner of your display to reveal the Control Center, and then touch the Camera icon.

❖ Swipe left on your iPhone's Lock screen.

Note: For your safety, a green dot will appear in the upper right corner of your display when the Camera is being used.

Take a picture

Enter the Camera application, then touch the Shutter or press any of the volume buttons to capture a photo.

Switch between camera modes

Swipe to the right or left on your camera screen to pick any of the following camera modes:

- ❖ Video: Record a video.
- ❖ Timelapse.
- ❖ Slo-mo: Record a slow-motion video.
- ❖ Pano: Snap a panoramic landscape.
- ❖ Portrait.
- ❖ Cinematic: Apply immersive effects to your video.
- ❖ Square: Take a photo with a square aspect ratio.

Zoom in or zoom out

- ❖ Pinch open on your Camera screen to zoom in and pinch closed to zoom out.
- ❖ Toggle between 0.5 x, 1 x, 2 x, 2.5 x & 3 x to zoom in or out. For an accurate zoom, long-press the zoom controls, then drag the slider to the left or right.

Turn the flash on or off

Your phone camera will automatically use the flash when necessary. Before taking a picture, do the following for manual control:

Touch the Flash button⚡ to turn the flashlight on or off. Touch Click the Camera Controls icon⌃, and then touch the Flash button⚡ under the frame to select off, on, or Auto.

Capture a picture with a filter

Use filters to add colour effects to your photos.

❖ Enter the Camera application, swipe to Photo or Portrait mode, then touch the Camera Controls icon⌃, then touch the Filters icon🎨.
❖ Swipe left or right to see filters under the viewer; touch one to use it.

Use the timer

Set a timer to give yourself time to get in the shot.

To set a timer, enter the Camera application, Touch the Camera Controls icon⌃, tap the Timer icon⏱, select 3s or 10s, and then touch the Shutter to begin the timer.

Page | 137

Take a Live Photo

Live Photo snaps what takes place before & after you snap your picture as well as the sound.

❖ Enter the Camera application.
❖ Ensure the Camera is in Photo mode and Live Photo is enabled.
 When Live Photo is turned on, you will see the Live Photo icon ◎ at the upper part of your camera screen. When you see a Slash in the Live Photo icon it means that the Live Photo is off. Touch the icon to activate or deactivate Live Photo.
❖ Touch the Shutter to snap a Live Picture.
❖ To play the Live Picture, touch the picture thumbnail at the lower part of your display, then long-press your screen to play it.

Take action photos with Burst mode

With Burst mode, you can capture moving subjects, or capture many high-speed pictures so that you have a range of pictures to select from. You can use the front & back camera to take burst photos.

❖ Enter the Camera application.

❖ Swipe the Shutter button to the left

The counter will display the number of photos you have taken.

❖ Raise your finger to stop.

❖ To choose the pictures you want to save, touch the Burst thumbnail, and then touch the **Select** button.

Gray dots under the thumbnails indicate recommended images to save.

❖ Touch the circle in the bottom right corner of each picture you want to store as a separate picture, and then touch the **Done** button.

To delete the whole Burst, touch the thumbnail, and then touch the Trash icon 🗑 .

Take a photo with your front camera

❖ Enter the Camera application.
❖ To switch to the front camera, touch the Camera Selector button ⊚ to switch to the front camera
❖ Place your phone in front of you.
❖ To snap a photo or record, touch the Shutter or press any of the volume buttons.

To capture a selfie that takes the shot as you see it on the front camera, instead of reversing it, enter the Settings application> Camera, then activate Mirror Front Camera.

Take macro pictures & videos

Your iPhone makes use of the Ultra Wide camera to capture macro photos – stunning close-ups with sharp focus.

- ❖ Enter the Camera application, then swipe to video or photo mode.
- ❖ Go near the subject – as close as 2cm. Your iPhone camera will automatically switch to the Ultra Wide lens.

- ❖ Touch the Shutter to snap a picture or the Record button to record a video.

Capture a macro slow-motion or time lapse video

- ❖ Enter the Camera application and swipe to Time Lapse or Slo-mo mode.
- ❖ Touch .5x to use the Ultra Wide camera, then go close to the subject.
- ❖ Touch the Record to begin & stop recording.

Control automatic macro switching

You can control when your camera automatically uses the Ultra Wide camera for taking macro pictures & videos.

❖ Enter the Settings application, touch Camera, and then activate Macro Control.
❖ Enter the Camera app, and then go close to your subject
When you enter the macro range of your subject, you will see a Macro icon ✿ on your screen.
❖ Touch the Macro icon ✿ to deactivate automatic macro switching.

❖ Touch the Macro icon  to activate automatic macro switching.

Capture a picture in portrait mode

Portrait mode applies a depth-of-field effect that keeps your subjects— pets, persons, etc.—sharp while blurring the background & foreground.

❖ Enter the Camera application and then swipe to Portrait mode.
❖ Adhere to the directives on your screen to frame the object in the yellow portrait box.
❖ Drag the Portrait Lighting Control icon⬡ to select a lighting effect:
  ➢ Natural light.
  ➢ Studio Light
  ➢ Contour Light
  ➢ Stage Light.
  ➢ Stage Light Mono
  ➢ High-Key Mono
❖ Touch the Shutter to snap the photo.

After taking a picture in Portrait mode, you can turn off the portrait mode effect if you do not like the effect. Open a picture in the Photos application, touch the Edit button, and then touch the **Portrait** button to activate or deactivate the effect.

Capture Apple ProRAW pictures

Apple ProRAW combines standard RAW format data with iPhone image processing to provide more creative control when you adjust exposure, colour & white balance.

Set up Apple ProRAW

Page | 145

To setup Apple ProRAW, enter the Settings application> Camera > Formats and then activate Apple ProRAW.

Note: Apple ProRAW images store more information about the images, which would result in bigger file sizes.

Capture images with Apple ProRAW

❖ Enter the Camera application, then touch the ProRaw Off icon 🔘 to activate ProRAW.
❖ Take your shot.
   While shooting, you can toggle between the Raw On icon 🔘 and the Raw Off icon 🔘 to activate or deactivate ProRAW
   To save your ProRAW settings, enter the Settings application> Camera > Preserve Setting and then activate Apple ProRAW.

Change the Apple ProRAW resolution

You can take ProRAW pictures in 12MP & 48MP.

❖ Enter the Settings application> Camera > Formats.

❖ Activate Apple ProRAW, touch ProRAW Resolution, then select 12MP or 48MP.

Adjust the shutter volume on your camera

While in the Camera app, open the Controls Centre, and then drag the volume slider 🔊 to change the sound level.

Record a video

❖ Enter the Camera application and then swipe to Video mode.
❖ Touch the Record button or press any of the volume buttons to start recording. When recording, you can:
  ➢ Press the white Shutter to take a picture.
  ➢ Pinch open on your Camera screen to zoom in and pinch closed to zoom out.
  ➢ Toggle between 0.5 x, 1 x, 2 x, 2.5 x & 3 x to zoom in or out. For an accurate zoom, long-press the zoom controls, then drag the slider to the left or right

❖ Touch the Record button or press any of the Volume buttons to stop the recording session.

Use Action mode

Action mode improves stabilization when recording in video mode. Touch the Grey Action Mode icon ⊛ at the upper part of your display to activate Action mode and touch the Yellow Action Mode icon ⚹ to deactivate it.

Record a QuickTake video

A Quick-Take video is a video recorded in Photos mode. If you're recording a QuickTake video, you can move the Record button to the locked position and continue taking still pictures.

❖ Enter the Camera application in Photos mode, then long-press the Shutter to start a QuickTake video recording.
❖ Slide the Shutter to the right and lift your finger when it's in Lock position for hands-free recording.

➢ Touch the White Shutter button to snap a picture while recording.

➢ Swipe up to zoom in on your subject, or if you're recording manually, you can pinch open on the screen to zoom in.

❖ Touch the Record button to stop recording.

Touch the thumbnail to check out the Quick-Take video in the Photos application.

Record a slow-motion video

When recording a video in Slomo mode, the video is recorded as normal and you can see the slow motion effect when you play it. You can also edit your video to start slow motion and stop it at a fixed time.

❖ Enter the Camera application and then swipe to Slo-mo mode.

You can touch the Camera Selector button ⊙ to record with the front-facing camera.

❖ Touch the Record button or press any of the volume buttons to start & stop recording.

To slow down part of the video and play the rest at normal speed, touch the video thumbnail and then touch the **Edit** button. Drag the vertical bar under the frame viewer to specify the segment you want to play in slow motion.

Record a video in Cinematic mode

The Cinematic mode uses depth-of-field effects that keep the subject of the video sharp while creating beautifully blurred surfaces and backgrounds. The iPhone automatically detects the subject of the video and keeps it in focus during recording; iPhone automatically moves the focus point when a new subject is detected. You can also manually adjust the focus point while recording or edit it later in the Photos application.

❖ Enter the Camera application, then swipe to Cinematic mode.

To change the depth effect, touch the Adjust Depth icon 🄵 and then drag the slider to the right or left before you record.

❖ Touch the Record button or press any of the volume buttons to record.
  ➢ A yellow frame on your display indicates the person in focus; the gray color frame indicates that someone else has been detected, but not in focus. Touch the grey frame to change the focus; touch the frame once more to close the focus on that individual.
  ➢ If there's nobody in the video, touch anywhere on your screen to set the focus point.
  ➢ Long-press your screen to lock the focus on a point.
❖ Touch the Record button or press any of the volume buttons to stop recording.

Check out our pictures

❖ Enter the Camera application, and then touch the thumbnail in the bottom left corner of your screen.
❖ Swipe to the right or left to view your recent pictures.
❖ Touch the screen to hide or display the controls.

❖ Touch the **All Photos** button to check out all your pictures & videos stored in the Photos application.

Share & print your pictures

❖ View checking out a picture, touch the Share icon ⬆.
❖ Choose an option to share your pictures, such as Messages, Mail, or AirDrop.
❖ To print your picture, choose Print from the Actions list.

Use Live Text with your camera

The camera can copy, share, search, and translate text found in the camera frame.

❖ Enter the Camera application, then set your phone in a way that the text can be seen in the camera frame.
❖ When a yellow frame appears around the visible text, touch the Live Text icon ⬚ and then carry out any of the below:

> Copy text
> Select All: Select all the visible text

- Look-Up View: Show specific website recommendations.
- Translate: Translate the text.
- Search the web
- Share: Share text via Messages, AirDrop, or other options.

Note: You can also long-press the text, then select specific text with the grab points to perform the actions listed above.

❖ Touch the Live Text On icon to go back to Camera.

To deactivate Live Text on your phone camera, enter the Settings application> Camera, then deactivate Show Detected Text.

Scan the QR code with your camera

❖ Enter the Camera application, then set your phone in a way that the code can be seen on your screen.
❖ Touch the on-screen notification to access the appropriate site or application.

FACETIME

The FaceTime application can help you to stay in touch with loved ones, whether they are making use of Apple devices or not.

Setup FaceTime

❖ Enter the Settings application, touch Face-Time, insert your Apple ID & password in the appropriate fields, and then touch the **Sign In** button.
❖ Ensure FaceTime is activated, then carry out any of the below:

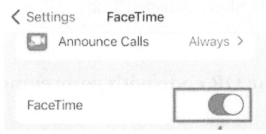

➢ Watch videos together, listen to songs together, or share your screen in a call: Touch SharePlay, then activate SharePlay.
➢ Show live captions in a call: Activate Live Captions.
➢ Take a Live Photo in Face-Time calls: Activate Face-Time Live Photos.

➢ Make natural eye contact in FaceTime calls: Activate Eye contact.

Make FaceTime calls

With connection to the Internet, you can make & receive FaceTime calls.

Turn off your mic.

Turn off your camera.

Drag your image to any corner.

Add stickers and other fun effects.

Switch to the rear camera.

Take a Live Photo.

❖ In the FaceTime application, touch the **New FaceTime** button.

❖ Enter the phone number or name of the person you want to call in the input field, then touch the FaceTime Video button to make a video call or the FaceTime Audio button to make a voice call.

Or, touch the Add Contact icon to enter the Contacts application and add someone from there; or touch a contact in your call history to make a call.

Receive FaceTime calls

When someone calls, carry out any of the below:

❖ Accept a call: Touch the Accept button.
❖ Reject call: Touch the Decline button.
❖ Touch the Remind button to create a reminder to call the person back.
❖ Touch the Message button to send an SMS to the person.

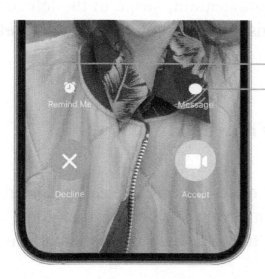

Set up a reminder to return the call later.

Send the caller a text message.

Start a FaceTime call from a Message chat

In a Message chat, you can begin a Face-Time call with the person you are having a conversation with.

- ❖ Touch the FaceTime button at the upper right part of the Message chat.
- ❖ Carry out any of the below:
  - ➤ Touch the **FaceTime Audio** button.
  - ➤ Touch the **FaceTime Video** button.

Delete a call from your call history

In the FaceTime application, swipe to the left on a call in your call history and then touch the **Delete** button.

Create a FaceTime call link

You can create a link to a Face-Time call and send it to a person or a group of people (via Mail or Message), which they can use to participate in a FaceTime call.

- ❖ In the FaceTime application, touch the **Create Link** button.
- ❖ Select an option to send the link (Mail, Message, etc.).

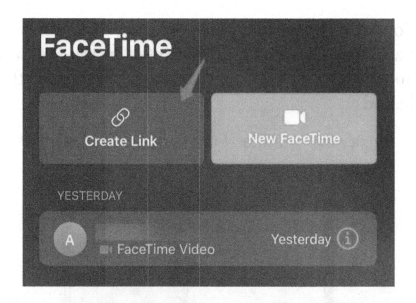

You can invite anybody to join a Face-Time call even those that do not have an Apple device. They can join the call from their browser, no login required.

Take a Live Photo

While making a FaceTime video call, you can take a Live Picture to capture a moment of the call. The camera snaps everything that takes place before & after you take the picture, as well as the sound so that you can see & hear it just as it happened.

To take Face-Time Live Photos, first ensure FaceTime Live Photos is activated in the Settings application> FaceTime, then carry out any of the below:

❖ In a one-on-one FaceTime call: Touch the Capture button ◯.

Take a Live Photo.

❖ On a Group call: Touch the tile of the individual you want to take a photo with, touch the Full Screen button , then touch the Capture button ◯.

The two of you will get notified when the photo has been taken, and the Live Picture will be stored in the Photos application.

Use Live Captions in a FaceTime call

While making a FaceTime video call, you can use Live Captions to see your discussion transcribed on your display. If you have trouble hearing what the other person is saying in the call, the Live Caption feature can make it easier to follow along.

❖ While on a video call, touch your screen to display the controls (if they're not already visible).

❖ Touch the Info button ⓘ at the upper part of the controls, activate Live Captions, then touch the **Done** button.
A Live Caption window will appear, displaying the transcribed dialog at the upper part of your display.

To stop using Live Captions, touch your screen, Touch the Info button ⓘ at the upper part of the controls, then deactivate Live Captions.

Use other applications while on a FaceTime call

While making a FaceTime call, you can use other applications—for instance, to perform a calculation or to search for info.

Page | 165

Swipe up from the lower edge of your display to go to the home screen, then touch an application to launch it.

To go back to the Face-Time display, touch the green bar at the upper part of your display.

Make a group FaceTime call

In the Face-Time application, you can have about 32 participants in a group call.

❖ In the FaceTime application, touch the **New FaceTime** button.

❖ Enter the phone numbers or names of the individuals you want to call in the input field, then touch the FaceTime Video button to make a video call or the FaceTime Audio button to make a voice call.

Or, touch the Add Contact icon to enter the Contacts application and add someone from there; or touch a contact in your call history to make a call.

Everyone participating in the call will appear in a tile on your screen. When someone starts speaking or you touch a tile, that tile will become more prominent. Scroll down to find a participant you can't see.

To stop the speaker's tile from becoming larger during a Group call, enter the Settings application> FaceTime, then deactivate Speaking in the Automatic Prominence section.

Add someone to a call

❖ While on a call, touch your screen to display the controls (if they're not already visible). Touch the Info button ⓘ at the upper part of the controls, and then touch the **Add People** button.

- ❖ Enter the phone numbers or names of the individuals you want to call in the input field,

  Or, touch the Add Contact button ⊕ to add a person from your contacts list.
- ❖ Touch the **Add People** button.

Leave a Group call

Touch the **Leave** button to leave a group call.

Share your screen in a FaceTime call

You can share your screen in a Face-Time call, to bring applications, websites, and more to the discussion. You can discuss about what you are working on, collaborate on a document with other people in the call, and view a picture album while seeing & hearing how others react in the call.

❖ While on a call, touch your screen to display the
controls (if they're not already visible), touch the

Share Content icon, then touch the **Share My Screen** button

❖ Carry out any of the below:

➢ Share your screen: Touch an application under Apps for SharePlay.

➢ Show a document or application: Swipe up from the lower edge of your display to go to the home screen, then touch an application you want to share in the FaceTime call.

Your screen will appear in the conversation for everybody to see after 3 seconds

To stop screen sharing, touch the Share content icon.

Handoff a Face-Time call to another Apple device

You can move a FaceTime call to another device that uses your Apple ID.

Note: The contact info selected for the call, displayed in the Settings application> FaceTime (under You Can Be Reached At), has to match the contact info selected in the Settings application> FaceTime for the device you want to handoff to.

❖ Ensure your other device is switched on, and then touch the screen that is showing the call.
The call notification will appear on the other device along with the prompt "Move the call to [device]".

❖ To switch the call, touch the notification or touch the Video Handoff icon at the upper left part of your display, then touch the Switch icon
The call screen will appear, displaying the camera, MIC, and sound settings.

❖ Ensure the camera, mic, and sound settings are what you want, then touch the Switch icon .
The call will move to your other device. A banner will appear on the original device confirming that the call has been moved to the other device, as well as the Switch icon , which you can touch to bring the call back to the original device.

Blur your background

With Portrait mode, your iPhone can blur your background and put the visual focus on you.

❖ While on a Face-Time call, touch your tile.

❖ Touch the Portrait icon 🔵 in your tile.
Touch the icon once more to deactivate Portrait mode.

Turn Portrait mode off or on.

Switch to the back camera

While on a Face-Time call, tap your tile, and then touch the Switch Camera icon 📷.

Touch the icon 📷 once more to return to the front-facing camera.

Note: when making use of the back camera, you can zoom in by touching 1x. Touch it again to return the image to its normal size.

Turn off the camera

While on a call, touch your screen to display the controls (if they're not already visible), then touch the Video icon .

Touch it once more to turn on the Camera

Filter out background noise

If you want the other people in the call to hear your voice clearly during FaceTime calls, you can activate Voice Isolation mode. Voice Isolation mode makes your voice the priority in a FaceTime call and blocks out the background noise.

While on a FaceTime call, swipe down from the upper right corner of your screen to open the Controls Center, touch MIC mode, and then choose Voice Isolation.

If you want others in the call to hear your voice and the sounds around you in a FaceTime call, you can activate Wide Spectrum

Turn off the sound

While on a call, touch your screen to display the controls (if they're not already visible), then touch the sound icon to mute yourself.

Touch the icon once more to turn on the sound

Become a Memoji

In the Messages application, you can create Memoji characters to use in Face-Time calls. Your phone will capture your gestures, facial expressions & voice and transfers them to your character.

❖ While on a FaceTime call, touch the Effects icon . (If you can't see the Effects icon , touch your screen.)

❖ Touch the Memoji icon , then select a Memoji.
   The other person in the call will hear what you're saying but sees the Memoji talking.

Use filters to change your looks

* While on a FaceTime call, touch the Effects icon 🏵. (If you can't see the Effects icon 🏵, touch your screen.)
* Touch the Filters icon 🎨 to open the filters.
* Choose your look by touching one of the filters at the lower part of your screen (swipe to the right or left to see all of them).

Leave a call

Touch your screen to display the FaceTime controls, then touch the Leave Call icon ⊗.

Block unwanted FaceTime callers

You can block Face-Time calls from unwanted callers in the Face-Time application.

* In your Face-Time call history, touch the Info icon ⓘ beside the name, number, or e-mail of the contact you want to block.

❖ Scroll down, touch the **Block this Caller** button and then touch the **Block Contact** button.
❖ Choose the contact.

To unlock a contact, touch the Info icon beside the name of the contact, number, or e-mail in your call log, scroll down, and then touch the Unblock this Caller button.

SAFARI

You can surf the internet; translate web pages, preview sites link, and more in the Safari application.

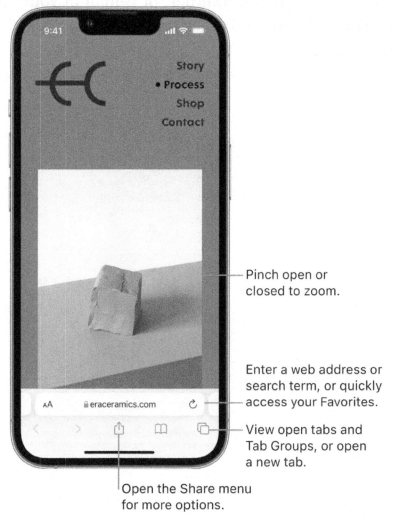

Pinch open or closed to zoom.

Enter a web address or search term, or quickly access your Favorites.

View open tabs and Tab Groups, or open a new tab.

Open the Share menu for more options.

Search for sites

❖ Type a phrase, URL, or search term in the search bar.

❖ Touch one of the search suggestions, or touch the **Go** button on your keyboard to look for what you've typed.

View sites in Safari

You can surf through a page with few taps.

❖ Return to the top of a page: tap the upper edge of your display two times to quickly go back to the beginning of a long page.

❖ Refresh a webpage: drag down from the upper edge of the web page.

❖ Share a link: Touch the Share icon ⬆ at the lower part of the webpage.

Preview site links

Long press a link in the Safari application to preview it without having to open the webpage. To open the link, touch the preview, or select Open.

Touch anywhere outside the preview to close it and remain on the webpage you are in

Touch and hold a link to see the URL and these options.

Translate an image or page

When viewing a page or image in another language, Safari can help you to translate the text.

Touch the Page Format icon AA, then touch the Translation icon .

Customize your start page

The Start page is the page you see when you open a new tab. You can personalize your start-page with new images & options.

- ❖ Touch the Share icon , then touch the New Tab icon $+$.
- ❖ Scroll down to the end of the page, and then touch the **Edit** button.
- ❖ Select an option for your page.
  - ➢ Use the Start page on all devices signed in with your Apple ID.
  - ➢ Tab Group Favorites: view & open tabs you have tagged as favourites.

> Recently closed tabs: check out your newly closed tabs.

- ➢ Favourites: Show shortcuts to your favourite bookmarked sites.
- ➢ Siri Suggestions.
- ➢ Frequently Visited: Go directly to your most visited sites.
- ➢ Privacy Report:
- ➢ Reading list: see sites in your reading list.
- ➢ Background image: Change your start page background image.

Change the text size

- ❖ Touch the Page Format icon AA in the search bar.
- ❖ Touch the Big **A** to increase the size of the font or the small **A** to reduce the font size.

Change display

Touch the Page Format icon AA in the search bar, then carry out any of the below:

- ❖ Visit a page without advertisements or a navigation menu: Touch the **Show Reader** button.

❖ Hide the search bar: Touch the **Hide Tool Bar** button (touch the top of your display to show it).

❖ See how the site looks on a desktop computer: Touch the **Request Desktop site** button.

Change your Safari layout

In Safari, you can choose the style that suits you best. Depending on the layout, the search bar will appear at the upper part or at the lower part of your display.

Enter the Settings application, touch Safari, and then scroll to Tabs. Choose Single Tab or Tab Bar.

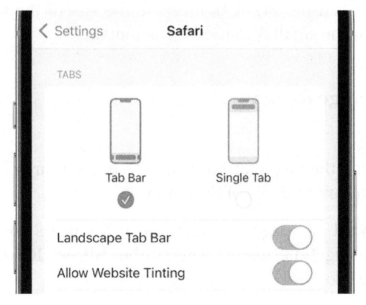

Search a page

You can look for a specific word or phrase on a page.

❖ Touch the Share icon, and then touch the **Find on Page** button.
❖ Type a phrase or word in the search bar.
❖ Touch the Mentions icon ∨ to go to other places where the word or phrase is mentioned.

Open a link in a new tab

You can use tabs to navigate between many open web pages.

To open a link in a new tab, long-press the link, then touch the **Open in New Tabs** button.

To remain in the tab you are in any time you open a link in another tab, enter the Settings application> Safari > Open Link, and then touch In Background.

Check out a tab's history

You can check out the sites you've visited in a tab. Long-press the Back button ‹ or the Forward button › in the tab.

Close a tab

Touch the Tabs button ⧉, then touch the Close button ⊗ in the top right part of a tab to close the tab.

Tip: To close all the tabs in the Group at once, long-press the **Done** button, then touch Close All Tabs.

Open a tab you recently closed

Touch the Tabs button ⧉, long-press the New Tab button +, and select from the closed tabs list.

Create a new Tab Group

In Safari, you can create Tab Groups to help organize your tabs and make it easy to find them later.

❖ Touch the Tabs button ⬚ to see all your tabs.
❖ Long-press a tab, then select the **Move to Tab Group** button.
❖ Touch the **New Tab Group** button, and name the Tab Group.

Tip: To move from one Tab Group to another, touch the Tab Groups button ⌄ in the bottom middle of your display.

Rearrange tabs in a Tabs Group

❖ Touch the Tabs button ⬚ to see all your tabs in that Tab group.
❖ Long-press a tab.
❖ In the pop-up menu, touch the **Arrange Tabs By** button, and then select an option.

Pin a tab

You can pin a tab to the top of the Tabs Group.

❖ Touch the Tabs button ⬚ to see all your tabs in that Tab group.
❖ Long-press the tab.

❖ In the pop-up menu, touch the **Pin Tab** button.

Move a tab to a different Group

❖ Long-press the Tabs button ⬜, then touch the **Move to Tab Group** button.
❖ Select any of the Tab Groups you've created earlier or create a new tab group.

Bookmark a website

Long Press the Bookmarks icon 📖, then touch the **Add Bookmark** button.

View & organize your bookmarks

❖ Touch the Bookmarks icon 📖.
❖ Touch the **Edit** button, and then carry out any of the below:
  ➢ Create a new folder: Touch the **New Folder** button at the lower left, name the folder, then touch the **Done** button.
  ➢ Delete a bookmark: Touch the Delete icon ●.
  ➢ Change the name of a bookmark: Touch the bookmark, rename it, then touch the Done button.

> Rearrange bookmarks: Long-press the Edit icon 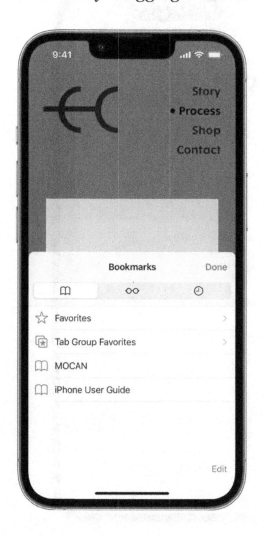, then move the bookmark to another location by dragging it there.

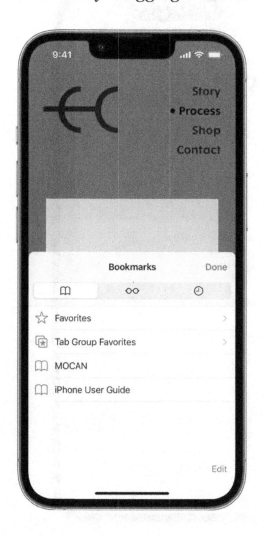

Hide advertisements & distractions in Safari

Readers view configures web pages to display only relevant text & pictures.

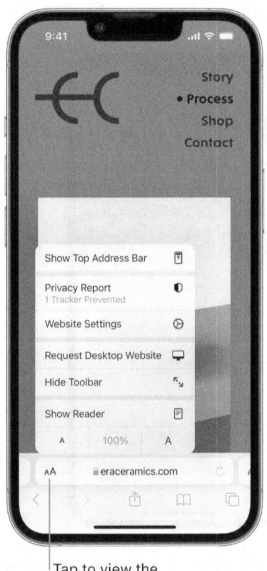

Tap to view the page in Reader.

Touch the Page Format icon AA, and then touch the **Show Reader** button.

To leave the Readers view, touch the Page Format icon AA, then touch the **Hide Reader** button.

Block pop-ups

Enter the Settings application> Safari, and then activate **Block Pop-ups**.

Browse privately in Safari

With Private Browsing mode, you can open tabs that do not appear in your iPhone's History

❖ Touch the Tabs icon 🗗 .
❖ Touch the Groups Tab icon ⌄ in the middle of the tabbar at the lower part of your display, and then touch the Private button

To verify that you are in Private Browsing Mode, simply check the search bar is gray or showing the word Private.

To hide a page and leave Private Browsing Mode, touch the Tabs icon ⬜, then touch the Tab Groups icon ⌄ to open another Tab group. The Private Websites will appear when next you make use of Private Browsing Mode.

To close a private tab, touch the Tabs icon ⬜, then swipe to the left on the tab you plan to close.

Clear your cache

You can clear your browsing data & history to clear the cache on your phone. This will remove the history of sites you've visited. This step will also remove the cookies & permissions you've given to sites to use your location or send you messages.

❖ Touch the Bookmarks icon 📖, then touch the History icon 🕐.
❖ Touch the **Clear** button in the lower right part of your screen, then select how much of your history to delete.

PHONE & CONTACT

To make a phone call in the Phone application, dial the phone number on the keypad, touch a recent call, or select a phone number from your contact list.

Dial a Phone number

❖ In the Phone application, touch the Keypad button.

Make the call on another line.

❖ Carry out any of the below:
  ➢ Use another line: touch at the upper part of the app, then select another line.
  ➢ Type the Phone number with your keypad: if there is an error in what you typed, touch the Erase button ❌ .
  ➢ Insert a "+" for international calls: Long-press the "0" button until you see "+".

❖ Touch the Call key 📞 to make the call.

Touch the End Call button ☎ to end a call.

Call someone from your favourites list

❖ Touch the **Favourites** button to select someone to call.
❖ To manage your favourites list, carry out any of the below:

  ➢ Add favorites: Touch the Add icon ➕ , then select one of your contacts.
  ➢ Touch the **Edit** button to delete or rearrange your favourites.

Redial a recent call

❖ Touch the **Recents** button, then call someone from there

❖ Touch the More details button $\textcircled{i}$ to get more information about the call & the person that called.
A red icon shows the number of missed calls.

Call somebody on your contact list

❖ In the Phone application, touch the **Contacts** button.
❖ Touch a contact and then touch the number you want to call.

Answer a phone call

Carry out any of the below:

❖ Touch the Accept button

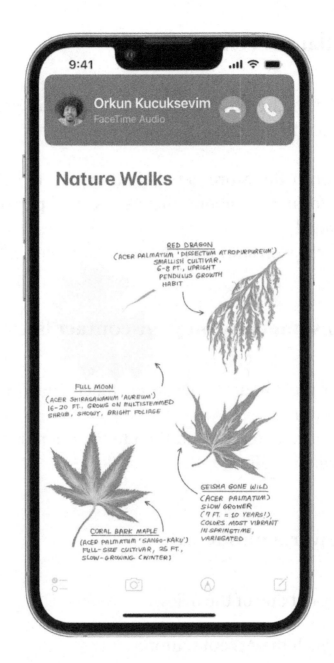

❖ Drag the slider if your phone is locked

Silence a call

Press the side key or any of the volume buttons.

Decline calls

Carry out any of the below:

❖ Double-press the side button.
❖ Touch the Reject Call button .

Swipe down on the banner to see more options

Adjust the audio while on a call

Press the volume button on your phone to change the volume level. Or swipe the call banner down, then carry out any of the below:

❖ Mute: Touch **Mute**.
❖ Put the call on hold: Long-press the Mute button.

Start a conference call

You can setup a conference call with about 5 people (depending on your network operator).

❖ While on a call, touch the **Add Call** button, make another phone call, and then touch the **Merge Call** button.
  Follow the steps above to add others to the call
❖ While on the conference call, carry out any of the below:
  ➢ Talk to someone privately: Touch the More info icon ⓘ, then touch the **Private** button

beside the person. Touch the **Merge Call** button to continue the conference call.

> ➢ Add an incoming call to the conference call: Touch the **Hold Call + Answer** button, then touch the **Merge Call** button.

> ➢ Drop someone: Touch the More info icon ⓘ beside the person, then touch the **End** button

Set a different ringing tone for a contact

❖ Enter the Contacts application ▣ .

❖ Choose one of your contacts, touch the **Edit** button, then touch the **Ringtone** button, and then select a ringing tone.

Block calls & messages from certain people

Carry out any of the below in the phone application.

❖ Touch the **Recents, Favourites, or Voicemail** button. Touch the More info icon ⓘ beside the number or contact you plan on blocking, scroll down, and then touch the **Block this Caller** button.

❖ Touch the **Contacts** button, touch the contact you plan on blocking, scroll down, and then touch the **Block this Caller** button.

Manage your blocked contacts

❖ Enter the Settings application> Phone > Blocked Contacts.
❖ Touch the **Edit** button

Create a contact

In the Contacts application , touch the Add button .

Find a contact

In the Contacts application , touch the search bar at the upper part of your contacts list, then type the contact's name, address, number, or other info.

Share contacts

Touch one of your contacts, touch the **Share Contact** button and then select a method to send the contact details.

Quickly reach a contact

To compose a message, make a call, start an e-mail, or send money to someone via Apple Pay, touch a button under the name of the contact.

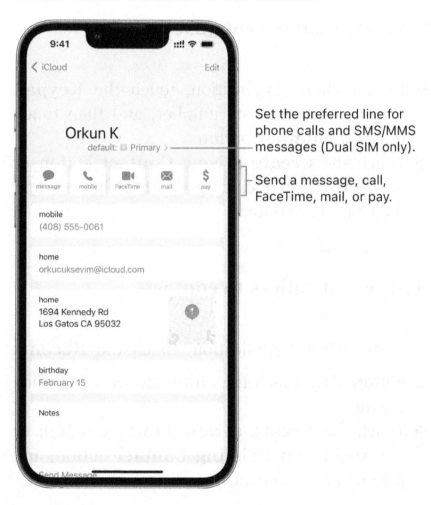

Set the preferred line for phone calls and SMS/MMS messages (Dual SIM only).

Send a message, call, FaceTime, mail, or pay.

Delete a Contact

* Touch the **Edit** button in the contact's card.
* Scroll down and then touch the **Delete Contact** button.

Save the number you just dialed

* In the Phone application, touch the **Keypad** button, type a phone number, and then touch the **Add Number** button.
* Touch the **Create a New Contact** button or the **Add to an Existing Contact** button, and then choose a contact.

Add recent callers to contacts

* In the Phone application, touch the **Recents** button, then touch the More info icon ⓘ beside the number.
* Touch the **Create a New Contact** button or the **Add to an Existing Contact** button, and then choose a contact.

APP STORE

In the Application Store, you'll find new applications, exclusive stories, tips & tricks, and in-application events.

Note: You need an Internet connection to use the Application Store.

Find applications

Touch any of the below:

- ❖ Today: Check out stories, applications & in-application events.
- ❖ Games
- ❖ Apps.
- ❖ Arcade: Enjoy a collection of promotional games from Apple Arcade (subscription needed) without advertisements or in-application purchases.
- ❖ Search: Type what you want, then touch the **Search** button on your keyboard.

Learn more about an application

Touch an application to view the following info & more:

- ❖ Screenshots
- ❖ In-application event
- ❖ Reviews & ratings
- ❖ Compatible languages
- ❖ Game Center Support
- ❖ Support for other Apple devices
- ❖ Size of file
- ❖ Privacy details

Buy & download an application

- ❖ Touch the price. Touch the **Get** button if the application is free.

    If a Redownload button ⬇ is displayed instead of a price, it means that you've already purchased the application and can download it for free.
- ❖ If necessary, authenticate with Face ID or your login code to finish the purchase.

Share or give an application

❖ Touch the application to view its details.

❖ Touch the Share icon⬆, then select a sharing option or touch the **Gift App** icon.

Redeem or send an Apple Gift card

❖ Touch the My Account icon⬤ or touch your profile photo in the upper right.
❖ Touch any of the below:
  ➢ Redeem Gift Cards or Codes
  ➢ Send Gift cards by E- mail

INTERACT WITH TEXT & SUBJECTS IN PICTURES

While viewing a picture in the Photos application, you can interact with the subjects & text that appear in the picture.

Use Live Text

❖ Open a picture or pause a movie that has text in it.

❖ Touch the Live Text icon⟨⟩, and then long-press the highlighted text.

❖ select specific text with the grab points, and then carry out any of the below:
  ➢ Copy text.
  ➢ Select All: Highlight all the text in the frame.
  ➢ Look-Up View: Show specific website recommendations.
  ➢ Translate: Translate the text.
  ➢ Search the web
  ➢ Share: Share text via Messages, AirDrop, or other options.

Depending on the photo's content, you can touch a quick action at the lower part of your display to make a call, visit a site, compose an e-mail, etc.

❖ Touch the Live Text icon 🔳 to go back to the video or picture.

Use Visual Look Up

Get more information about birds, landmarks, sculptures, pets, plants, art, & insects that appear in your pictures.

❖ Open an image; The Visual Look Up icon ⓘ implies that Visual Lookup info is available for that picture.

❖ Touch the Visual Lookup icon ⓘ or swipe up on the picture.

❖ Touch the icon that pops up in the picture or at the upper part of the picture info window to check out Siri Knowledge & more details about the object.

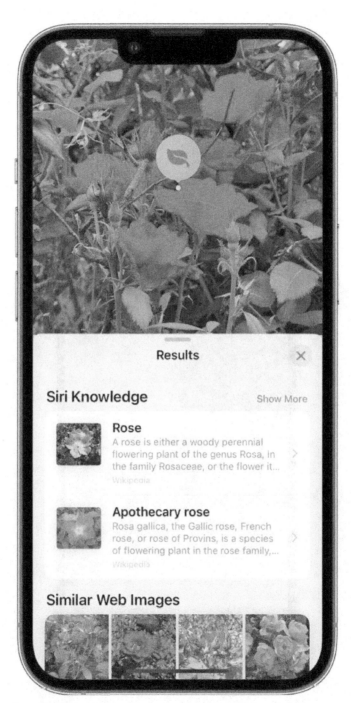

Lift a subject from the picture background

You can lift subjects of pictures away from their backgrounds in other to copy & share them in other documents & applications.

❖ Open a picture.
❖ Briefly long-press the subject of the picture. When it's highlighted, carry out any of the below:
  ➢ Touch the **Copy** button, then paste the subject into an e-mail, note, text message, etc.
  ➢ Touch the **Share** button, then select a sharing option (Mail, AirDrop, etc.)

MAIL

In the Mail application, you can add e-mail accounts to send & receive e-mails, and remove e-mail accounts that you don't need anymore.

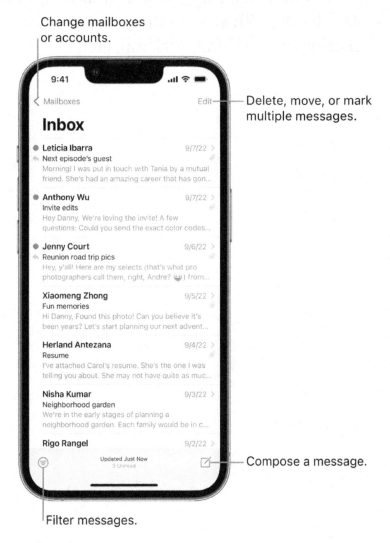

Change mailboxes or accounts.

Delete, move, or mark multiple messages.

Compose a message.

Filter messages.

Add an email account

When you launch the Mail application for the first time on your phone, you may be prompted to setup an email account—simply adhere to the directives on your screen.

To add more e-mail accounts, adhere to the directives below:

❖ Enter the Settings application> Mail > Account > Add Accounts.

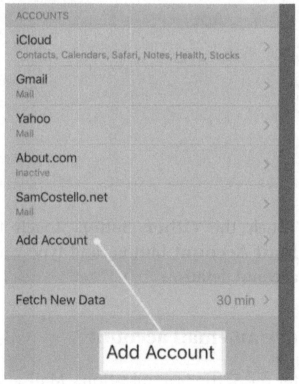

❖ Carry out any of the below:

➢ Touch an e-mail service - for instance, iCloud or Google mail - and type your e-mail account details.

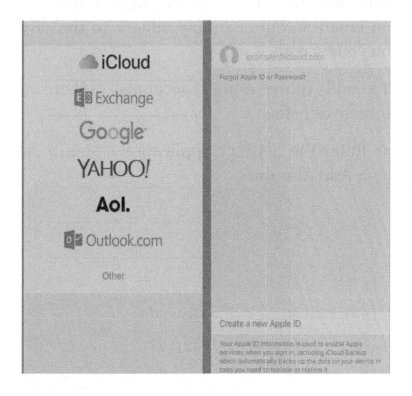

➢ Touch the **Other** button, touch the **Add Mail Account** button, and type your e-mail account details.

Remove an email account

❖ Enter the Settings application> Mail > Account.

❖ Touch the e-mail account you plan on removing, then carry out any of the below:
  ➢ If you want to remove an iCloud e-mail account: Touch iCloud, touch iCloud Mail, and then deactivate **Use on this iPhone**.
  ➢ If you want to remove another e-mail account: Disable Mail.
  Note: To delete the account from all iPhone applications, touch the **Delete Account** button.

Read an e-mail

In your mail Inbox, touch an email to read it.

Remind Me

If you can't handle an e-mail right away, you can schedule a date & time to get a reminder and bring the message to the upper part of the mail inbox.

Touch the More Actions icon ↰, touch the **Remind Me** button, then select when you want to receive the reminder.

Preview an e-mail

If you want to check out what's in an e-mail, without opening it completely, you can preview the email. In your mail inbox, long-press an email to view its content

Send an email on your iPhone

You can write & edit emails from your email account

❖ Touch the Edit icon ☑ .
❖ Touch in the e-mail, then write what you have in mind.
❖ To make changes to the format, touch the Expand Toolbar button ‹ at the top of your keyboard, and then touch the Text Format button Aa .
  Change the font style & text colour, add a numbered or bullet list, etc.
❖ Touch the Send icon ⬆ to send the e-mail.

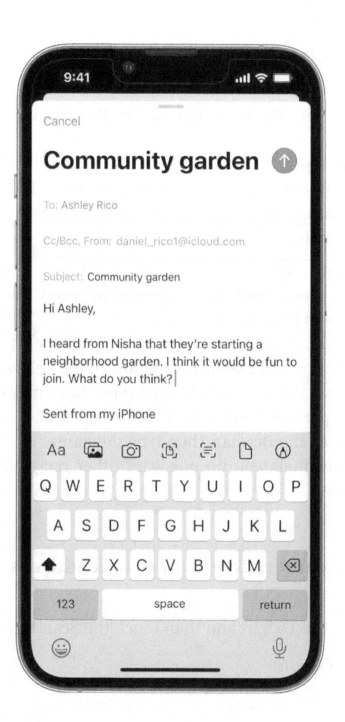

Add recipients

❖ Touch the **To** bar, then enter the recipient's name.
While typing, the Mail app will automatically suggest people in your Contacts, as well as the e-mail addresses for people that have multiple email addresses.

You can also touch the Add Contact icon ⊕ to enter the Contacts application and add recipients from there.

❖ If you plan to send a copy to others, touch the Bcc/Cc bar and then carry out any of the below:
  ➢ Touch the Cc bar, and then type the names of the persons you want to send a copy to.
  ➢ Touch the Bcc bar, then type the names of the individuals you do not want other recipients to see.

Use the camera to get an e-mail address

❖ Touch the To bar, and then touch the Scan Email Address icon ⊡.

❖ Set your phone in a way that the address can be seen on your screen.

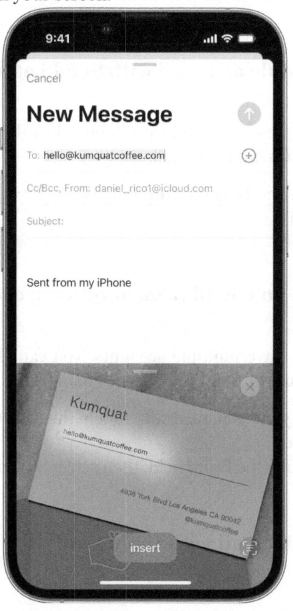

❖ When you see a yellow frame around the visible text, touch the **insert** button.

Schedule an email with Send Later

Long-press the Send icon, then select the time you want to send the e-mail.

Touch the **Send Later** button to check out more options.

Send an e-mail from another account

If you have multiple accounts, you can choose the account you want to send the email from.

❖ In your e-mail draft, touch the Bcc/Cc, From field.
❖ Touch the From field, then select an account.

Recall email with Undo send

The Mail application allows you to unsend an e-mail.

After you send an e-mail, you have 10 seconds to change your mind and unsend it.

Touch the **Undo Send** button at the lower part of your display to unsend an email

You can give yourself more than 10 seconds to change your mind and unsend an email by setting a delay, simply enter the Settings application, touch Mail, touch the **Undo Send Delay** button, then select how long you want to delay outgoing emails.

Reply to an email

❖ Touch in the e-mail, touch the Reply icon ↰, and then carry out any of the below:
  ➢ Touch the **Reply** button to reply to the person that sent the email.
  ➢ Touch the **Reply All** button to reply to the sender & other recipients.
❖ Write what you have in mind

Add pictures, documents, or videos to an email

You can add & send docs, videos, and images to your e-mail.

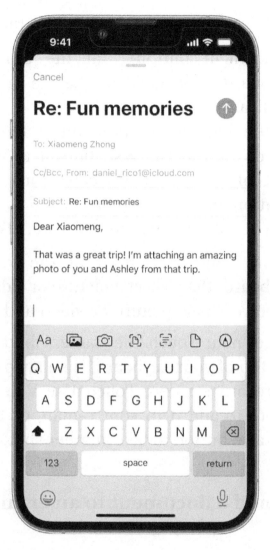

❖ Touch in the email, then touch the Expand Tools
   button ‹ at the top of your keyboard.
❖ Carry out any of the below:

➢ Add a document: Touch the Insert Attachment button ⬚ at the top of your keyboard, then look for the file in the Files application.

In the Files application, touch the **Recent** button or the **Browse** button at the lower part of your display, then touch a folder, location, or file to open it.

➢ Add a saved video or picture: Touch the Insert Photo button 🖼 at the top of the keyboard, then select a picture or video.

➢ Capture a new picture or video and add it to the e-mail: Touch the Camera button 📷 at the top of your keyboard, then snap a picture or record a video. Touch Use Video or Use Photo to add it to your e-mail, or touch the **Retake** button to take another shot.

Scan & add a document to an email

You can scan a doc and send it in PDF format.

❖ Touch in the email, then touch the Expand Tools button ‹ at the top of your keyboard.

❖ Touch the Scan Document button⬛ at the top of your keyboard.

❖ Set your phone in a way that the document can be seen on your screen— your phone will automatically capture the document.

To manually snap the document, touch the Shutter⭕ or press any of the volume buttons.

Touch the Flash settings icon⚡ to turn the Flashlight on or off.

❖ Touch the **Retake** button or the **Keep Scan** button, scan more pages, then touch the **Save** button when you are done.

❖ To edit the saved scan, touch it, then carry out any of the below:

➤ Touch the Crop icon ⊐ to crop the picture.

➤ Click the Show Filters icon 🔵 to apply Filters.

➤ Touch the Rotate button⬜ to rotate the document.

➤ Touch the Delete button🗑 to delete the document.

Download an attachment sent to you in an email

Long-press the attachment, then touch Save to Files or Save Image.

If you touched Save to Files, you can find the file in the Files application. if you touched Save Image, you can find it in the Photos application.

Tip: Touch the **Share** button to open the attachment with another application.

Search for an email in the Mail application

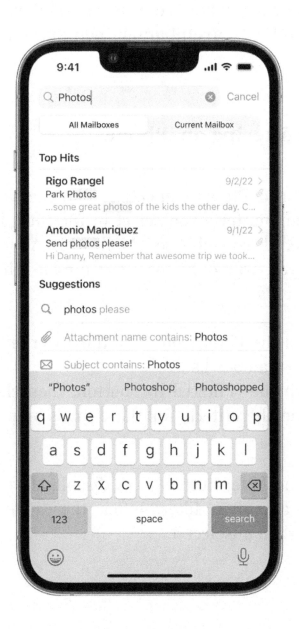

❖ In the mailbox, drag down to open the search bar, touch it, then write the text you want.
❖ Touch All Mailboxes or Current Mailbox.
❖ Touch the **Search** button, then touch an e-mail in the list of results to read it.

Email filtering on iPhone

You can use filters to quickly display messages that match any criteria you select in the filter list. For instance, if you choose "Mail with Attachments Only", you will only see your e-mails that have attachments.

❖ Touch the Filter icon ⊜ in the lower left corner of the mail box list.
❖ Touch the "Filtered by" button, then choose or enable the criteria for the e-mails you want to see.

Touch the Filter button ⊜ to disable all filters. To disable a certain filter, touch the "Filtered by" button, then unselect it.

Use Mail Privacy Protection

You can activate Mail Privacy Protection to make it difficult for senders to get info about your email activities. To protect email privacy, it hides your IP address from the sender, so that they cannot link it to your other online activities or pinpoint your location. It also stops email senders from knowing if you have opened the e-mail they sent.

❖ Enter the Settings application, touch Mail, then touch Privacy Protection.
❖ Activate Protect Mail activities.

Delete an email

There are many ways to erase e-mails. Carry out any of the below:

❖ While checking out an e-mail: Touch the More Actions button ↰, then touch the Trash icon 🗑.
❖ In your email list: Swipe left on the email, then touch the **Trash** button from the menu.
❖ Delete many e-mails at once: In the email list, touch the **Edit** button, choose the e-mails you plan on deleting, and then touch the **Trash** button.

Recover deleted emails

❖ Touch the Back button ‹ in the top left part of your display, then touch the Trash mail box of an account.
❖ Touch the email you plan on recovering, then touch the More Actions icon ↰.
❖ Touch the **Move Message** button, then select another mail box.

Print an e-mail

Touch the More Actions icon ↰ in the e-mail, then touch the **Print** button.

Print attachments or images

Touch an attachment, touch the Share button ⬆, and then select Print.

MAPS

You can see your location on a map and zoom in to find the needed information in the Maps application.

Let the Maps app use your location

To find your location & give correct directions, your phone has to be connected to the Internet and Precise Location has to be enabled.

❖ If the Maps application shows a message that Location Services is disabled: Touch the message, touch Turn On in Setting, then activate Location Services.
❖ If the Maps application shows a message that Precise Location is disabled: Touch the message, touch Turn On in Setting, touch Location, turn activate Precise Location.

Show where you are on the map

Touch the Locate icon � .

You will see your current position in the center of the map. At the top of the map is the North. If you want the Maps app to display where you are heading at the top instead of north, touch the Headings icon ◥ . Press the Directional Control key ⋀ or the Compass icon ⁿ to start showing north.

Pick the correct map

The icon at the upper-right part of a map indicates whether the map is for sightseeing ▮▮▮ , driving 🚗 , bus 🚌 , or satellite view 🌐 . To use another map, adhere to the directives below:

❖ Touch the icon at the upper right part of the map.
❖ Select another type of map, then touch the Clear icon ✕ .

View a 3D map

Carry out any of the below on a 2D map:

❖ Swipe up with 2 of your fingers.
❖ Touch the 3D button at the upper right part of a Satellite map.
❖ In selected cities, touch the 3D button at the upper right.

You can carry out any of the below on a 3D map:

❖ Drag 2 of your fingers down or up to change the angle.

❖ Zoom in to check out buildings and other small features.
❖ Touch the 2D button to go back to a 2D map.

Move, zoom or rotate a map or globe

❖ Drag the map to move around it.
❖ Zoom in or out: Pinch open to zoom in on a map. Pinch closed to zoom out
❖ Rotate a map: Long-press the map with 2 of your fingers, then rotate your fingers.
❖ Explore the world with a 3D globe: Keep zooming out on a map until it turns into a globe. Drag the map to move around it, zoom in or out to see details for oceans, mountains, deserts, etc.

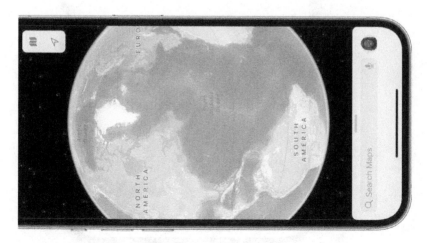

Search for a place

Touch the search bar, then type what you want.

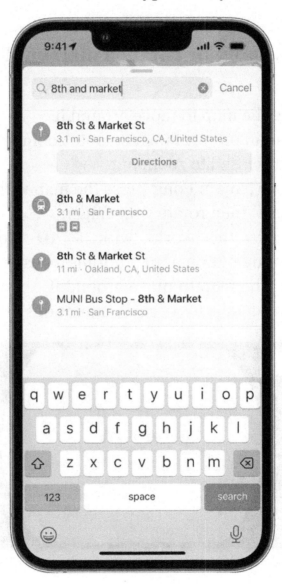

You can search in many ways. For instance:

❖ Crossroads ("7th & Market")
❖ Area ("Damascus Town")
❖ Place (Stonehenge)
❖ ZIP Code ("69322")
❖ Business (restaurants in London, movies, etc.)

Touch any of the results to get more information or receive directions to the place.

TRANSLATE

You can translate voice, text, & discussion between all supported languages in the Translate application. You can download languages for full translation on your phone, even without connecting to the internet.

Translate your voice or text

❖ Touch the **Translation** button, choose the languages, and then carry out any of the below:
  ➢ Touch the **"Enter text"** button, write a phrase, then touch the **Go** button.
  ➢ Touch the Listen icon 🎤 , then speak.
❖ When you see the translation, carry out any of the below:
  ➢ Touch the Play icon ▶ to play the translation.
  ➢ Touch the Favorite icon ☆ to add the translation to your favourites.
  ➢ Touch the Full Screen icon ↘ so that others can see the translation clearly.

Tip: Swipe the translation down to see your translation history.

Translate a conversation

❖ Touch the **Conversation** button.
❖ Touch the Listen icon 🎤 , then speak in any of the 2 languages.

You can translate a discussion without touching the MIC before each person talks. Touch the More Options icon ⋯, touch the **Auto-Translate**

button, and then touch the Listen icon ⬇ to begin the discussion. Your phone will automatically detect when you start and stop talking.

When having a face-to-face conversation, touch the View Chat icon ▭ , then touch the **Face to Face** button so that everyone can view the chat from the side.

Download languages for offline translation

- ❖ Enter the Settings application, and touch Translate.
- ❖ Touch the **Downloaded Languages** button, then touch the Download icon ⬇ beside the language you plan on downloading.

APPLE PAY

You can use Apple Pay to securely pay for things in
stores, applications, & sites that are compatible
with Apple Pay.

Add a credit or debit card

❖ In the Wallet application, touch the Add Card icon ⊕. You may be prompted to log in with your Apple ID.
❖ Carry out any of the below:
  ➢ Add a new card: Touch Credit or Debit Card, touch the **Continue** button, then Set your card in a way that the details can be seen in the frame on your screen, or insert the information manually.
  ➢ Add your old card: Touch the **Previous Cards** button, then select a card that you have used before. These cards can include cards that you've removed, cards associated with your Apple ID, etc. Touch the **Continue** button, verify with Face ID, and insert each card's CVV number.

Your card provider will determine whether your card is qualified for Apple Pay and may ask you for more details to finish the verification process.

Choose a default card and reorganize your cards

- ❖ In the Wallet application, select the card you want to use as your default card.
- ❖ Long-press the card, then move it to the front of the card's stack by dragging it there.
- ❖ To change the location of any other card, long-press the card, then move it to another location by dragging it there.

Find places that accept Apple Pay

You can use Apple Pay for safe, contactless payments in restaurants, stores, etc.

You can use Apple Pay anywhere you see these payment logos:

Pay for items with the default card

❖ Press the side button twice quickly.
❖ When you see your default card, stare at your phone to confirm with Face ID or insert your passcode.
❖ Put the top of your phone close to the card reader and wait until you see Done and a confirmation icon on your screen.

Pay with a different card

❖ Press the side button twice quickly.
❖ When you see your default card, touch it, then select any other card
❖ Stare at your phone to confirm with Face ID or insert your passcode.
❖ Put the top of your phone close to the card reader and wait until you see Done and a confirmation icon on your screen.

Use Apple Pay in applications, Applications Clips, and Safari

You can pay for items you purchased in applications, Application Clips, or on online using Safari with Apple Pay.

❖ When checking out, touch the **Apple Pay** button.
❖ Go through your payment details and set any of the below:
  ➢ Credit card
  ➢ Shipping & Billing Address
  ➢ Personal information

❖ Press the side button twice quickly, then stare at your phone to confirm with Face ID or insert your passcode.

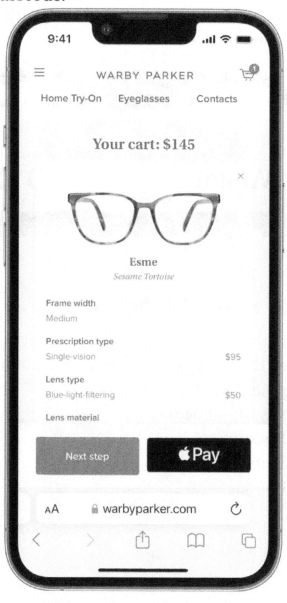

Track your orders

In the Wallet application, touch the Orders icon  to view the order information, shipping status, etc.

Change your information

- ❖ Enter the Settings application, and touch Wallet & Apple Pay.
- ❖ Set any of the below:
  - ➤ Email
  - ➤ Shipping address
  - ➤ Phone

APPLE CARD

The Apple Card is a credit card designed by Apple to help you live a healthy financial life. You can register for an Apple Card in the Wallet application and start making use of the card with Apple Pay in stores, applications, or online

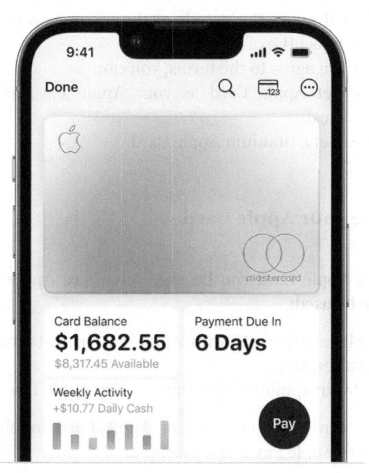

Get an Apple Card

❖ In the Wallet application, touch the Add Card
   icon ⊕ , then touch the **Apply for Apple Card**
   button.
❖ Insert your details, and then accept the terms &
   condition.
❖ Go through the details of the offer, then accept
   or reject the offer.
❖ If you agree to the terms, you can:
   ➢ Set Apple Card as your Apple Pay default
      card.
   ➢ Get a titanium Apple Card

Use your Apple Card

The Apple Card can be used anywhere Apple Pay
can be used:

❖ Make payments with Apple Pay in restaurants,
   stores, etc.
❖ Pay in applications or online with Apple Pay

You can also make use of Apple Card in places
where Apple Pay is not accepted:

❖ In the applications, online, or on your phone: Touch the Card Number button to view your card's number, expiry date, and security code. You can buy things with this info

❖ In shops, restaurants, and other places: Make use of the Titanium card.

View transactions & statements

❖ In the Wallet application, touch Apple Card.
❖ Carry out any of the below:
  ➢ Go through your transactions: scroll down to check out your transactions. You can also search for a transaction by touching the Search icon, after that type what you are looking for in the search bar, and touch search on your keyboard.
  ➢ View yearly, monthly, or weekly activities: Touch Activity in the Card Balance section to see what you have spent. Touch Year, Month, or Week to get a different view.
  ➢ Get a monthly report: Touch the **Card Balance** button to check out your new spending, balance & payments.

Pay for things

Touch the Payments button. Or, touch the More icon ⊙, touch card details, then select one of the below:

* ❖ Scheduled payments: Select Pay Different Amounts or Pay My Bills, insert the details of your payment (like the date & account, then confirm with Face ID, or password.
* ❖ Pay for an item: Touch the **Show Keyboard** button to add the amount, touch the **Pay Now** button or the **Pay Later** button, go through your details (like payment account), and authorize with Face ID or password.

SIRI

With Siri, you can perform tasks on your phone using just your voice. You can tell Siri to translate a sentence, set alarms, find locations, provide weather reports, etc.

Your iPhone has to have internet connection before Siri can perform certain tasks.

Setup Siri

Enter the Settings application, touch Siri & Search and then carry out any of the below:

❖ Activate **Listen for Hey Siri** if you want to use your voice to summon Siri
❖ Activate **Press Side Button for Siri** if you want to summon with a button.

Summon Siri

❖ Say "Hey Siri" or long-press the side button. When Siri appears, make your request

❖ To request for something else, touch the Listen icon or Say "Hey Siri" once more

Type instead of talking to Siri

❖ Enter the Settings application, touch Accessibility, touch Siri, and then activate Type to Siri.
❖ To make a request, summon Siri, then type what you want Siri to do for you

Change Siri settings

Enter the Settings application> Siri & Search, then carry out any of the below:

❖ Deactivate **Allow Siri When Locked** to restrict access to Siri when you lock your phone
❖ Change the Language Siri answers to: Touch Language, then choose another Language.
❖ Always see Siri response on your screen: Touch Siri Response, then activate Always Show Siri's Caption

❖ See your request on the screen: Touch Siri Response, then activate Always Show Speech

Change Siri's voice

You can change the voice of Siri

❖ Enter the Settings application, and touch Siri & Search
❖ Touch Siri's Voice, then select another voice or variety

NOTES

You can write quick ideas or organize detailed info with check-lists, pictures, links, documents, and more in the Notes application.

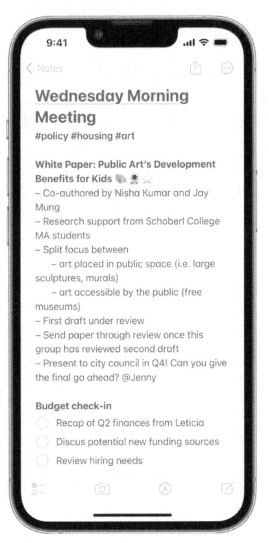

Create & format a new note

❖ Touch the New Note icon □ and then write what you want.
❖ Touch the Format icon Aa to make changes to the formatting.
  You can use heading styles, italic font, numbered lists, etc.
❖ Touch the **Done** button to save the note.

Tap on the Checklist icon ○— in the note to add a check list, after that simply type to enter text, and touch the return button to go to the next item.

Scan text into a note

You can upload scanned text in a note

❖ In a note, click the Camera button 📷
❖ Set your phone in a way that the text can be seen in the camera frame.
❖ When a yellow frame appears around the visible text, touch the Live Text icon 🔲
❖ Select the text you want with the grab points, then touch the **Insert** button

Scan a document

❖ In a note, click the Camera button 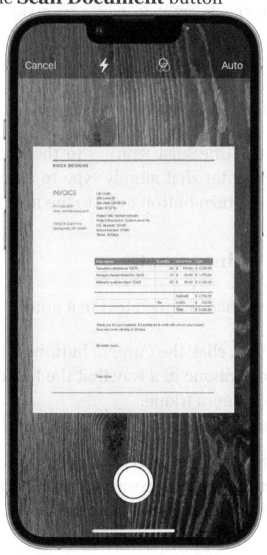, then touch the **Scan Document** button

❖ Set your phone in a way that the document can be seen on your screen— your phone will automatically capture the document.
To manually snap the document, touch the Shutter ○ or press any of the volume buttons.

Touch the Flash settings icon ⚡ to turn the Flashlight on or off.
❖ Scan more pages, then touch the **Save** button when you are done.
❖ To edit the saved scan, touch it, then carry out any of the below:

  ➢ Touch the Add icon ⊕ to add more pages

  ➢ Touch the Crop icon ⌐ to crop the picture.

  ➢ Click the Show Filters icon ⊗ to apply Filters.

  ➢ Touch the Rotate button ⟲ to rotate the document.

  ➢ Touch the Delete button 🗑 to delete the document.

Add a picture or video

❖ Touch the Camera icon 📷 in a note.

❖ Select a video or picture from your photos library, snap a new picture or record a video.

To store videos & pictures taken in the Photos application, enter the Settings application> Notes and then activate **Save to Photos**.

See all attachments in Notes

❖ At the top of the list of notes, touch the Folder Actions icon ⬭, and then touch the **View Attachments** button to view all your attachments.
❖ To enter a note with a specific attachment, touch the thumbnail of the attachment, then touch the **Show in Note** button

Create, rename, move, or delete folders

Carry out any of the below in the folder list:

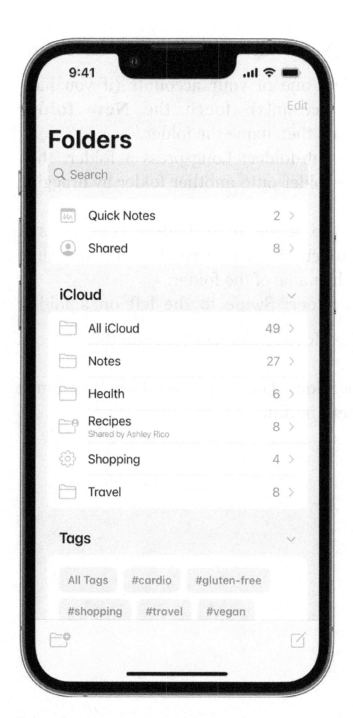

- ❖ Create a New folder: Click the New folder icon
  , select one of your accounts (if you have multiple accounts), touch the **New folder** button, and then name the folder.
- ❖ Create a sub-folder: Long-press a folder, then move the folder onto another folder by dragging it there.
- ❖ Change the name of a folder: Long-press a folder, touch the **Rename** button, and then change the name of the folder.
- ❖ Move a folder: Swipe to the left on a folder, touch the Move Folder icon , and then select a location.
- ❖ Delete a folder: Long-press a folder, then touch the **Delete** button.

CRASH DETECTION

If your phone detects a car accident, it can help in contacting emergency services & notifying your emergency contacts.

How Crash Detection works

When your phone notices a serious accident in your car, it will show a notification and automatically start calling emergency services after 20 seconds if you do not cancel the alert. If you do not respond, your phone will send a voice message to emergency services, informing them that you have been involved in a serious accident and it will also send them your longitudinal & latitudinal coordinates.

Enable or disable Crash Detection

Crash Detection is enabled by default. To deactivate it, enter the Settings application, touch Emergency SOS, then deactivate Call After Severe Crash.

MEDICAL ID

A Medical ID gives info about you that might be helpful in emergencies, such as medical conditions, allergies, & emergency contact information. Your phone can provide these details to the person attending to you in an emergency.

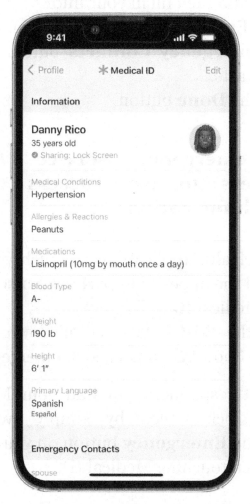

Setup your Medical Profile

❖ In the Health application 🤍 , touch your profile photo at the upper right part of your screen, then touch Medical ID

❖ Touch the **Get Started** button or the **Edit** button, and then fill in your info.

❖ In the Emergency Contacts section, touch the **Add Emergency Contacts** button, then add the contacts.

❖ Touch the **Done** button

Allow emergency service & first responders to gain access to your medical information

❖ In the Health application 🤍 , touch your profile photo at the upper right part of your screen, then touch Medical ID

❖ Touch the **Edit** button, scroll down, and then activate Show When Locked & Emergency Call.

Note: First responders can find your Medical ID from the lock screen by simply swiping up, touching the **Emergency** button on your passcode display, then touching Medical ID.

PASSCODE & FACE ID

Set a passcode

Set a passcode that has to be entered before your phone can be unlocked when you switch it on or wake it.

Set or change your passcode

- ❖ Enter the Settings application, then touch Face ID and Passcode.
- ❖ Touch the **Turn On Pass code** button or the **Change Pass code** button.
  Touch the **Passcode Options** button to check out options for setting up a password.

Adjust when your phone automatically locks

Enter the Settings application, touch Display and Brightness, touch Auto Lock, then set a time.

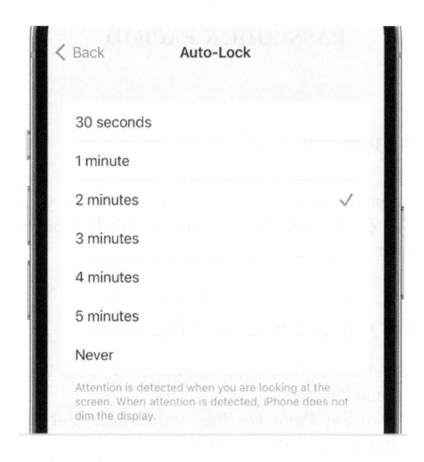

Erase your data after ten failed entries

Set your phone to delete all info, personal settings, & media after ten consecutive failed password entries.

❖ Enter the Settings application, then touch Face ID and Passcode.
❖ Scroll down and then activate Erase Data.

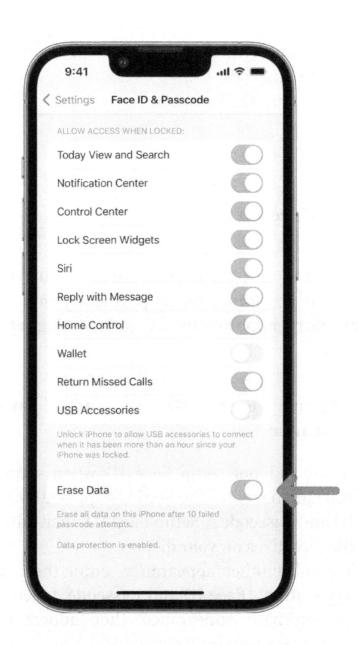

Disable the passcode

- ❖ Enter the Settings application, then touch Face ID and Passcode.
- ❖ Touch Turn Off Passcode

Setup Face ID

With Face ID, you can unlock your phone, authenticate purchases & payments, and access third-party applications by just staring at your phone.

Configure Face ID or add another appearance

- ❖ If you did not setup Face ID when setting up your phone, enter the Settings application> Face ID and Passcode > Setup Face ID, then adhere to the directives on your display.
- ❖ To add another appearance, enter the Settings application> Face ID and Passcode, touch Setup an Alternate Appearance, then adhere to the directives on your display.

Turn off Face ID

❖ Enter the Settings application> Face ID and Passcode.
❖ Carry out any of the below:
  ➢ Deactivate Face ID for certain things: deactivate any of the options.
  ➢ Deactivate Face ID: Touch the **Reset Face ID** button.

TURN ON/OFF, RESTART, UPDATE, BACKUP, RESTORE & RESET

Switch on your phone

Long-press the Side button till you see the Apple symbol.

Switch off your phone

Carry out any of the below:

❖ Long-press the Side button and any of the Volume buttons till the sliders pops-up, then slide the Power-Off slider.

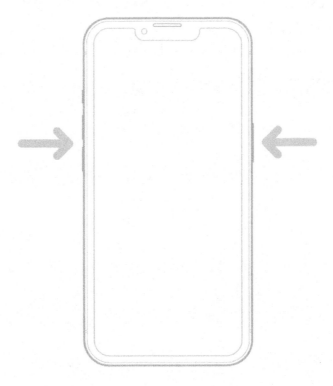

❖ Enter the Settings application, touch General, touch Shut Down, then slide the slider.

Force restart your phone

If your phone is unresponsive and you cannot switch it off, you can force it to restart.

❖ Press & release the Increase volume button quickly.
❖ Press & release the Reduce volume button quickly.
❖ Long-press the side button until you see the Apple Symbol

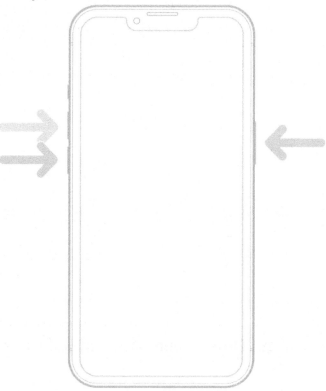

Update your iPhone's operating system

Before updating, ensure you backup your iPhone.

Update your phone automatically

❖ Enter the Settings application, touch General, touch Software Updates, then touch Automatic Update.
❖ Activate Download iOS Update
❖ Activate Install OS   Update.

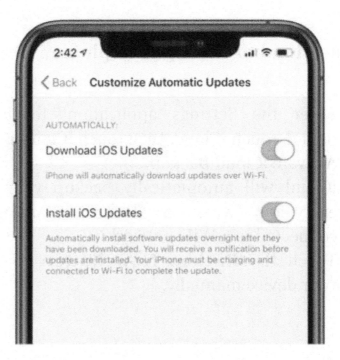

Update your phone manually

❖ Enter the Settings application, touch General, then touch Software Updates

Your screen will show the iOS version your phone is using and if there's an update available.

Backup your iPhone

Backup your iPhone with your PC or iCloud.

Use iCloud to backup your phone

❖ Enter the Settings application, touch [your name], touch iCloud, then touch iCloud Backup.
❖ Activate iCloud Backup.
   iCloud will automatically backup your phone every day when it's locked, charging, and connected to a WiFi network.
❖ Touch the **Backup Now button** to backup your device manually.

To check out your backups, enter the Settings application> [your name] > iCloud, touch Manage Accounts Storage, then touch Back Up. To remove a backup copy, select the back up copy from the list and then touch the **Delete and Turn Off Back Up** button.

Use your Mac to Backup your iPhone

* Use your USB cable to connect your phone to your mac.
* Choose your iPhone in your mac's Finder side bar.
* Click on **General** at the upper part of the Finder window.
* Choose **Backup all iPhone data to this Mac.**
* Select "Encrypt local back up" to encrypt and password-protect your backup.
* Click on the **Backup Now** button.

Use your Windows PC to Backup your iPhone

* Use your USB cable to connect your phone to your mac.

- ❖ In the iTunes application on your computer, click the iPhone button at the upper left part of the iTune window.
- ❖ Click on the **Summary** button.
- ❖ Click on the **Backup Now** button in the Backups section.
- ❖ To encrypt back up, choose "Encrypt backup", enter a passcode, and click on the **Set Password** button.

Restore all content from a backup

Restore your phone from an iCloud backup

- ❖ Switch on your new or just erased phone.
- ❖ Touch Setup Manually, touch Restore from iCloud Back Up, then adhere to the directives on your screen.

Restore your phone from a computer backup

- ❖ Use a USB cable to connect your new or just erased phone to the computer that has the backup.

❖ Carry out any of the below:
  ➤ On a Mac: Choose your iPhone in the side bar of the Finder, click on the **Trust** button, and then click on **Restore from this Back up**.
  ➤ On a Windows PC: Open iTunes, click on the iPhone icon at the upper left part of the iTunes window, click on the **Summary** button, and then click on the **Restore Back up** button.
❖ Select a backup from the list and click on the **Continue** button.

If the backup is password-protected, you must insert the login code before you can restore your settings & files.

Reset iPhone settings to defaults

You can return your phone settings to their defaults without deleting your content.

❖ Enter the Settings application, touch General, touch Transfer or Reset iPhone, then touch Reset.
❖ Select any of the below:

- ➢ Reset all settings
- ➢ Reset Network Settings
- ➢ Reset the keyboard dictionary.
- ➢ Reset Home Screen Layout.
- ➢ Reset location and privacy

Erase iPhone

Erase your iPhone to permanently delete your content & settings.

- ❖ Enter the Settings application, touch General, then touch Transfer or Reset iPhone.
- ❖ Select any of the below:
  - ➢ Prepare to move your contents to your new iPhone: Touch the **Get Started** button, then adhere to the directives on your screen. Once you're done, enter the Settings application> General > Reset iPhone and then touch the **Erase All Contents & Settings** button.
  - ➢ Erase all data from your phone: Touch the **Erase All Contents & Settings** button.

Made in United States
North Haven, CT
11 September 2023

41443527R00166

S0-EIA-185

Juv.
K79
My

8-85

My Friend Is Moving

by Christine Kohler
illustrated by Keith Neely

CONCORDIA®

Publishing House
St. Louis

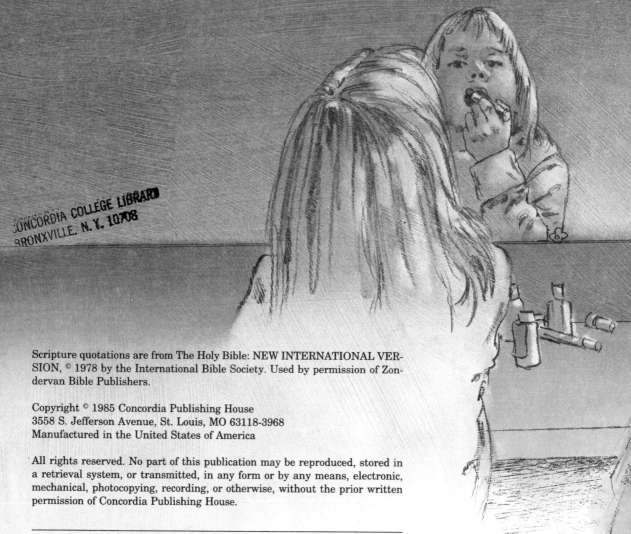

CONCORDIA COLLEGE LIBRARY
BRONXVILLE. N. Y. 10708

Scripture quotations are from The Holy Bible: NEW INTERNATIONAL VER-
SION, © 1978 by the International Bible Society. Used by permission of Zon-
dervan Bible Publishers.

Copyright © 1985 Concordia Publishing House
3558 S. Jefferson Avenue, St. Louis, MO 63118-3968
Manufactured in the United States of America

All rights reserved. No part of this publication may be reproduced, stored in
a retrieval system, or transmitted, in any form or by any means, electronic,
mechanical, photocopying, recording, or otherwise, without the prior written
permission of Concordia Publishing House.

Library of Congress Cataloging in Publication Data

Kohler, Christine, 1953-
   My friend is moving.

   (Growing up Christian series)
   Summary: Knowing they may not see each other again, Jennifer helps
her friend feel better about moving by reminding her that we remain firends
with Jesus even though we don't see Him.
   1. Children's stories, American. [1. Moving,
Household—Fiction. 2. Friendship—Fiction.
3. Christian life—Fiction] I. Title. II. Series.
PZ7.K82336My 1985   [E]   84-23062
ISBN 0-570-004116-3

1 2 3 4 5 6 7 8 9 10 DB 94 93 92 91 90 89 88 87 86 85

So far it had been a fun summer. Jennifer and Scotty Harper enjoyed playing with their friends every day. Curtis White lived next door to the Harpers in an old two-story house painted gold with black trim and shutters. They had been neighbors and best friends ever since they could remember.

On the other side of the Harper's house was a tall white house with green trim and a porch in front. Cindy Vercelli had lived there for about a year.

Jennifer and Cindy liked to play together. They would dress up in their mothers' old dresses and shoes and play house with their dolls. They also liked to jump rope and skip hopscotch and share secrets together.

Today Mrs. Harper had given them a nice long piece of clothesline rope, so all four children were taking turns jumping rope. Jennifer was taking her turn while Cindy watched and Curtis and Scotty twirled the ends.

They all chanted,

Teddy Bears, Teddy Bears by the ton.
Ma-Ma, would you buy me one?
Teddy Bear, Teddy Bear, be my friend;
We'll have fun, and we'll pretend.

Teddy Bear, Teddy Bear, play with me;
We'll swing high into the tree.
Teddy Bear, Teddy Bear, I love you.
Friends like you are fun but few.

How many Teddy Bears do you want?
One, two, three, four, five, six . . .

"Oops," said Jennifer, "I missed."

"My turn!" said Cindy.

"Cindy's turn takes too long," complained Scotty.

"That's because she's good," said Jennifer.

"After that I'll do 'hot peppers,'" offered Cindy.

Sure enough, Cindy skipped rope through the "Teddy Bear" rhyme plus ten more easily. When she counted eleven, Scotty and Curtis made the rope twirl real fast for "hot peppers."

" . . . eleven, twelve, thirteen, fourteen, fifteen . . ."

"Whew, I missed," said Cindy. "That was fun!"

"You are *good*," Scotty noted. "I have trouble just getting through the rhyme."

"Practice a lot, Scotty, and I'll teach you to do 'double dutch' with two ropes," said Cindy.

"If we can get another clothesline," said Jennifer.

Just then Cindy's father pulled into the driveway.

"Hey, I wonder why Daddy's home?" asked Cindy. "He's supposed to be working at the supermarket today."

"Maybe he came home for lunch," Jennifer offered.

"I don't think so," said Cindy. "Mommy always packs him a lunch."

"Speaking of lunch," Scotty added, "I'm hungry. Come on, Curtis; I'll race you to my house."

"Cindy," called Mrs. Vercelli, "come into the house now. We have some news to tell you."

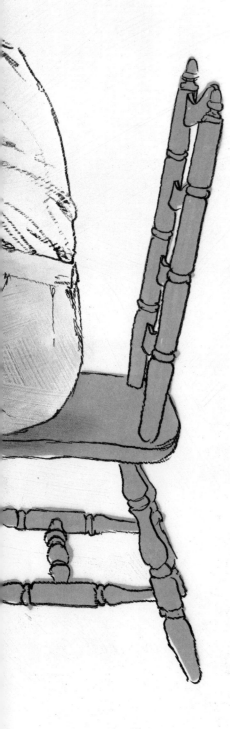

"Bye Cindy. Maybe we can play some more after lunch," said Jennifer.

"Bye Jenny. I'll see you later," Cindy called back as she hurried home.

When Jennifer got home, Mother was making peanut butter and honey sandwiches on whole wheat bread. On the table was a big bowl of fruit and a plate of carrots and celery. Scotty was helping Mother by setting the table.

"There you are, Jennifer," said Mother. "Go wash your hands now. Scotty's in a hurry to eat."

Jennifer washed her hands, then sat down at the table for lunch. Mother reached across the table and held Jennifer and Scotty's hands as they prayed this prayer together:

"Dear God,
Thank You for the food we eat.
Thank You for the friends we meet.
Thank You, Father, for Your Son,
Who is a Friend to everyone. Amen."

Usually Scotty ate his meals faster than Jennifer, but today Jennifer finished first.

"Why are you in such a hurry, Jennifer?" asked Mother.

"Cindy's daddy came home from work early today and her mommy said she had some news to tell her. I wonder if it could be a surprise!"

"Well," said Mother, "don't be rude and ask her what the news is. Wait until she volunteers to tell you."

"Okay," Jennifer agreed as she hurried out the door to Cindy's house.

Jennifer knocked on the screen door. When Cindy appeared she didn't look too happy.

"Can you come out to play, Cindy?"

"I don't want to." Cindy looked ready to cry.

Jennifer wanted to know what the news was and why Cindy was so upset, but remembered her mother told her not to ask. "If you want to play later, I'll be in the backyard."

Cindy shook her head no and went back into the house.

Jennifer waited all day for Cindy to come out and play. But Cindy never did.

The next morning Jennifer wanted to see if Cindy was feeling better. As Jennifer ran around the front of Cindy's house she saw a sign in the front yard. It read, FOR SALE.

"For Sale?" thought Jennifer. "Is Cindy going to move? Is that what the news is about?" Jennifer didn't see Cindy outside, so she went home to tell her mother about the "for sale" sign.

"Mommy, Mommy!" hollered Jennifer. "Guess what! There's a 'for sale' sign in front of Cindy's house."

"I know, dear," said Mother. "Mrs. Vercelli just called to tell me they will be moving soon."

"Why?"

"She said that her husband received a promotion. He's going to be the manager of a supermarket in another town."

"Why can't he be manager of this supermarket?" asked Jennifer.

"Because they already have a manager," said Mother. "Jennifer, we should be happy for the Vercelli's. This promotion is something Mr. Vercelli has worked very hard for. He is a good grocer—and his company must think so, too, in order to give him a promotion. We need to be happy for them even if we are sad they they will be moving."

"I don't think Cindy's happy about the promotion," said Jennifer.

"She will be," replied Mother. "It just may take some time. Do you remember how shy Cindy was when she moved here?"

"Yes," said Jennifer, "it took forever for her to come and play with me."

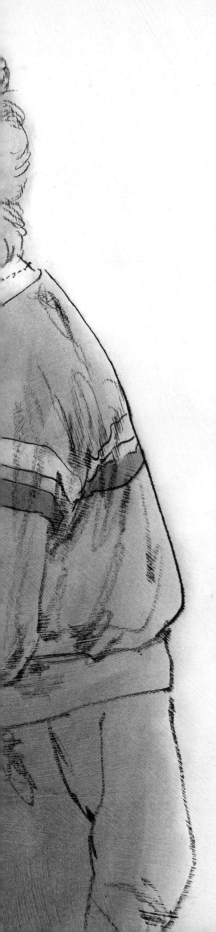

"Well, it wasn't exactly forever," Mother explained, "but it did take several weeks. That was because Cindy missed her old house and friends. Maybe she was afraid that if she made new friends she would have to say good-bye again."

"Do you think that's why she won't come out to play now?" asked Jennifer. "She doesn't want to say good-bye?"

"Something like that," Mother answered. "I think Cindy needs to know that you'll still be her friend, even if you don't see each other anymore. She also needs to be reassured that she will make new friends in her new town and that she can have fun with them, too."

"Will I ever get to see her again?" asked Jennifer.

"Maybe not," replied Mother. "In the Bible, when David and Jonathan parted for the last time, they never saw each other again. But they still remained friends."

"Maybe I could write Cindy letters," said Jennifer.

"That is a good idea," agreed Mother. "I thought perhaps you would like to make Cindy a going-away present."

"Anything to cheer her up," said Jennifer.

All morning Jennifer worked with Mother making a surprise going-away present for Cindy. After lunch Jennifer hurried over to Cindy's house to give her the surprise. Jennifer knocked on the door then waited and waited for Cindy. Finally Cindy answered the door. She still didn't look too happy.

"Jenny, I don't want to play today," said Cindy.

"Please come outside," Jennifer pleaded. "I have a surprise for you."

"A surprise? For me? What is it?" asked Cindy as she followed Jennifer out onto the porch.

"It's something I made. My mom helped me with the printing, but I drew all of the pictures by myself."

"Did you know we are moving?" asked Cindy, as the two girls sat on the steps.

"Yes," said Jennifer. "My mommy told me your daddy got a promotion."

"Daddy and Mommy are real happy about the promotion." Cindy commented.

"Are you?" asked Jennifer.

"Yes . . . and no," replied Cindy. "My insides are all mixed up. I'm happy Daddy was promoted, but I don't want to move. I like my bedroom with the daisies on the wallpaper and this porch with the old porch swing. Best of all I like playing jump rope and hopscotch with you—and Scotty and Curtis, too. I'm afraid I won't have a nice friend like you . . . ever again." said Cindy.

"My mommy says you will make a lot of new friends, Cindy." said Jennifer. "And we can still be friends, too."

"How can we be friends if we can't see each other anymore?" asked Cindy.

"I guess it is kind of like being friends with Jesus," said Jennifer. "He says that He loves us and we are His friends, but we don't see Him. Still, we know that Jesus is real. It's just that He has moved to heaven."

"I never thought about it that way," said Cindy.

"If you want, we could write letters, too," Jennifer offered.

"I don't write very well," said Cindy. Then she continued with a happier voice, "but my mom could help me." Cindy was much better now that she and Jennifer had talked about her feelings about moving.

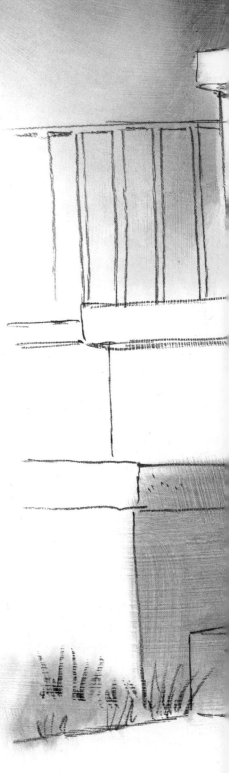

"Here's the surprise I made for you," said Jennifer.

"Oh, thank you!" Cindy exclaimed.

Jennifer handed Cindy a small package wrapped in the colored comic page from Sunday's newspaper. Inside was a little book Jennifer had made and stapled together. Cindy opened the pink construction paper cover to the first page. On the page was a picture of four children playing jump rope.

"That's supposed to be us jumping rope," said Jennifer. "See! That's you jumping. The boy with the short curly hair twirling the rope is Curtis. That's me with a skirt on, holding the other end of the rope. And that is supposed to be Scotty swinging on the tire swing under the tree."

"You drew this good, Jennifer," giggled Cindy. "I want to see the next page." Cindy turned the page. "Oh, look," said Cindy, "Bible verses."

"My mommy helped me find those," said Jennifer.

" 'There is a friend who sticks closer than a brother,' Proverbs 18:24," read Cindy.

"That includes sisters, too," said Jennifer. "See the picture. That is supposed to be you with a big smile on your face being friendly to another girl."

Cindy smiled big at Jennifer and Jennifer smiled back. They both laughed.

" 'May the Lord keep watch between you and me while we are away from each other,' Genesis 31:49," Cindy read from the third page. Underneath the Bible passage Jennifer had drawn a picture of Cindy and Jennifer waving good-bye. An angel was watching over them both.

"The rest of the pages are blank because it's an autograph book," said Jennifer. "My mom says an autograph book is where your friends are supposed to write nice things about you and sign their names. See? I printed my name and had Scotty and Curtis print their names, too. Then there are more pages left empty for your new friends to add their names." explained Jennifer.

"Oh, thank you, Jennifer! This is wonderful!" cried Cindy. "Wait here a minute. I have something I want to give you."

Cindy ran into the house and back out again with her mother's clothesline rope.

"Here. My mommy said I could give you her clothesline for a jump rope. I never got to teach Scotty double dutch. Now you have two ropes, so you can teach him."

Jennifer reached over and gave Cindy a big hug.

"I'm going to miss everything here, especially you," said Cindy. "But, I feel much better now about moving."

"Just remember," said Jennifer. "I will always be your friend. We can write, and you can tell me all about your new house and school and friends. And, remember most of all: Jesus promised to watch over us no matter where we live."